Mel Bay's MOUNTAIN DULCIMER

By Mark Biggs

A collection of traditional folksongs, Irish and American fiddle tunes, classical pieces, and original songs arranged and adapted for the mountain dulcimer with melody line and chords for other stringed instruments. Includes extensive tuning information and chord charts.

CD CONTENTS

1. Peppermint Stick Rag [2:17]
2. Tomorrow Today [2:25]
3. Sonya's Song [3:28]
4. Wildwood Flower/Old Joe Clark [2:52]
5. Nobody Home [3:05]
6. The Parting Glass [3:12]
7. Winter's Lament to Spring [2:32]
8. Farewell and Adieu Ye Fine Spanish Ladies [2:31]
9. The Ashgrove/Soldier's Joy [3:48]
10. Morning Song [3:59]
11. Greensleeves/ Lord Lovel/Drill Ye Tarrier's, Drill [4:30]
12. Ramble Away/What Do You Do With a Drunken Sailor [3:34]
13. Minuet in G (Bach) [2:24]
14. Munga Laten [2:50]
15. Sheebeg Sheemore [3:58]
16. The Touchstone/The Rakes of Mallow [3:14]
17. Old Molly Hare [2:03]
18. Star of County Down [4:11]
19. Golden Haired Maid in the Morning [2:53]

ACKNOWLEDGMENTS

I wish to especially thank Max Tyndall, a good friend and fine photographer, for all the time, patience, and energy he spent helping me prepare the photographs in this book. Likewise, I want to thank Jeff Doty of Memphis, Tennessee (a fine dulcimer player in his own right), for his superb guitar back-up on the Mel Bay recording which accompanies this book. In that vein, I wish to acknowledge and thank Steve Gardner of Columbia, Missouri, who was the recording engineer on my first album, *Not Licked Yet;* and Jim Walker of Air Trans Studios in Memphis, who was the recording engineer for the Selected Songs segment of this book. My special thanks to Lynn McSpadden and everyone at the Dulcimer Shoppe in Mountain View, Arkansas, where my fine hand-crafted dulcimers were built. Finally, I want to say thanks to all the folks at Mel Bay (especially Dean Bye) for their never-ending efforts on my behalf over the past year as they worked with me in putting this book together.

Mark Biggs, June 1, 1982

© 1982 BY MEL BAY PUBLICATIONS, INC., PACIFIC, MO 63069.
ALL RIGHTS RESERVED. INTERNATIONAL COPYRIGHT SECURED. B.M.I. MADE AND PRINTED IN U.S.A.
Visit us on the Web at http://www.melbay.com — E-mail us at email@melbay.com

TABLE OF CONTENTS

INTRODUCTION:
- To the Reader and Fellow Dulcimer Player 4
- No Wrong or Right Way to Play 5
- A Brief History of the Mountain Dulcimer 6
- A Few Words about Modes 7
- A Word about String Gauges 12
- How to Read the Numerical Tablature in this Book 12
- Placing Chords Behind the Melody Line 14
- Barre Chording with Your Little Finger 18

SONGS:

Part I: From *Not Licked Yet* 20
1. Peppermint Stick Rag 22
2. Tomorrow Today 24
3. Sonya's Song 25
4. Wildwood Flower 28
5. Old Joe Clark 29
6. Nobody Home 30
7. The Parting Glass 34
8. Winter's Lament to Spring (& Spring's Reply) 35
9. Farewell and Adieu Ye Fine Spanish Ladies 38
10. The Ashgrove 39
11. Soldier's Joy 40
12. Greensleeves 41
13. Lord Lovel 41
14. Drill Ye Tarrier's, Drill 42
15. Morning Song 44

Part II: Selected Songs 47
16. Ramble Away 48
17. What Do You Do With a Drunken Sailor 49
18. The Lass of Patie's Mill 50
19. Poor Wayfaring Stranger 51
20. Andante Grazioso (Mozart) 52
21. Minuet in G (Bach) 54
22. God Rest Ye Merry Gentlemen 56
23. Munga Laten 57
24. The Touchstone 58
25. The Rakes of Mallow 59
26. Old Molly Hare 61
27. Star of County Down 62
28. Sheebeg Sheemore 63
29. Golden Haired Maid in the Morning 64

Farewell and Adieu (All Ye Fine Dulcimer Players) 67
Glossary of Some Important Terms and Symbols 68
Reading Time Values 69
Chord Charts 72

Photo by Max Tyndall

Born in 1954, **Mark Biggs** began playing mountain dulcimer in 1979 when he and a friend found a job playing music for free room and board in a small Greek restaurant on the south side of Crete. He's come a long way from those first "ad lib" days, winning honors, contests and many listener's ears along the route. For the past three years he has played and demonstrated the dulcimer to hundreds of thousands of people at Silver Dollar City, an 1880's theme park in southwest Missouri. During this time he has competed in a number of dulcimer contests, placing:

    1980   1st—Midwest Dulcimer Championships—Council Bluffs, Iowa
    1981   1st—Southern Regionals—Mountain View, Arkansas
    1981   1st—Ozark Mountain Dulcimer Championships—Silver Dollar City, Missouri

Mark has taught dulcimer courses through the Continuing Education Departments at Drury College and Southwest Missouri State University in Springfield, Mo. Besides performing and teaching, he has begun to host a series of workshops and concerts throughout the Midwest in folkclubs, at festivals, and in centers of folklore preservation.

TO THE READER AND FELLOW DULCIMER PLAYER

I am constantly met with two basic reactions when people stop to watch me play the mountain dulcimer. One group stands by attentively silent, only to come forward afterwards to tell me how difficult it looks. The other faction just smiles and says how easy it looks. And not so oddly, both points of view are quite correct. Certainly the mountain dulcimer is a less complex instrument than the guitar or banjo. To begin with, you are dealing with a seven tone or modal scale instead of the normal modern twelve note octave or chromatic scale. Moreover, you are usually faced with only three or four strings. All of which means you have fewer chords in any one tuning to conquer, and less notes to deal with. Which is by no means necessarily a negative thing, for as Michael Murphy points out in the Appalachian Dulcimer Book, "The dulcimer, like any instrument, is characterized by its own limitations which lend to it a discernible quality." To my way of thinking it is a positive advantage that nearly anyone can pick up a dulcimer and within a few moments begin to make lovely personal music with it simply by running a noter or wooden dowel stick over the first string to lay down a melody line, using the remaining strings to form a constant droning background chord. Now while this traditional style of playing provides plenty of pleasing music, and was in fact the way I first began to explore the dulcimer some three years ago, this book is not intended as a mountain dulcimer primer. Rather, its aim is to show those of you who wish to lay your noters aside for the time being, or those of you already using your fingers how to add chords behind a melody line, and how to use octave and rhythm changes within a song to add as much life and feeling to a song as you desire, so that in the final analysis you can not only get more out of your dulcimer, but put more of yourself into your music.

NO WRONG OR RIGHT WAY TO PLAY

As far as I am concerned there are no right or wrong ways to play the mountain dulcimer; only harder and easier means to reach the same end. Because the mountain dulcimer has only recently begun to appear before the public's eyes, having been rescued from rural obscurity and near extinction by a renewed interest in folk music during the late fifties and early sixties, there exist no set playing styles, no decreed patterns to copy from or conform to; you are free to discover your own forms, to carry on the traditional music of the hills, or to forge your own personal music. In fact, I can't recall ever meeting two dulcimer players who played the same song in exactly the same way. Which is perfectly normal since no two people dance (or play) to the same tune, let alone share the same finger span or sense of timing. For instance, I never use my thumb when playing a song, content to utilize my four fingers and a technique of barre chording with my little finger (a procedure I'll describe in detail later on), whereas everyone else I've ever had the pleasure to play with has eventually brought their thumb into use. Yet neither the thumb nor not-to-thumb contingent may lay claim to being right or better; both methods produce beautiful renditions of the same song. The important thing to remember is that to play your best you must be both comfortable with and engaged by your own style, which means knowing your present physical limitations as well as your own abilities and ambitions. A certain equilibrium or balance is necessary to play the dulcimer, and not only to hold the slippery thing on your lap. The trick is to be both attentive and entertained; simultaneously relaxed and expectant. In order to prevent stagnation and boredom (with myself as much as with the dulcimer), I have found it essential to challenge myself constantly with new tunes and techniques, while remaining sensitive as to when to pull back and cement through repetition what I have learned. Every bit of fresh technique, each new song builds from what you already know and becomes the growing foundation for your future efforts. Don't be afraid to make mistakes or to try something outrageously different; don't shy away from a new tuning or a particularly difficult passage (what's hard today will certainly be easier tomorrow if you work on it); and <u>above all</u> don't let your frustrations get the better of you. Relax and enjoy, and those around you will also enjoy. Remember, there are no tried and true, wrong or right, sure fire ways to play the dulcimer; like everything else the instrument is only as complex or as simple as you choose to make it. And ultimately, the important thing is simply to get on with playing it.

Which is what this book is all about.

A BRIEF HISTORY OF THE MOUNTAIN DULCIMER

The Mountain or Appalachian Dulcimer (sometimes spelled 'dulcimore' by the mountain folk) is one of the few true American instruments; born, bred and most probably conceived sometime in the early 1800's, somewhere in the remote regions of the Appalachian mountains. Technically speaking the mountain dulcimer belongs to that family of instruments known as the plucked zither, and should not be confused with the hammered dulcimer, a large trapezoidal shaped, multi-stringed percussion instrument belonging in the psaltry family. Yet like this namesake cousin, the mountain dulcimer is a modal instrument, possessing an equally "sweet song", which is fitting since the word dulcimer comes to us from the Latin "dulce" for sweet, and the Greek "melos" for song. So it is understandable how the hill people who first built the mountain dulcimer chose this name, already familiar to them from its repeated mention in the Bible.

Historically a number of Renaissance instruments appear to form the model from which the modern mountain dulcimer acquired its unique shape. The oldest direct ancestor seems to have been the German scheitholt, a small three or four stringed monochord (all the strings tuned to the same note) plucked while a noter was run over the melody string. The scheitholt was being played over a wide region of Europe even before the turn of the 15th century, and as it grew in popularity became the prototype for a number of folk instruments including the French Epinette des Vosges and the Swedish humle. Like the mountain dulcimer all of these instruments were modal, and played flat on the lap or laid on a table. Nonetheless, the mountain dulcimer's shape (both the traditional 'hourglass' and 'teardrop' models) and its particular tone and string arrangement make it a unique instrument, clearly the outgrowth of a composite of these forerunners rather than the direct descendant of any single forefather.

A FEW WORDS ABOUT MODES

As I have already said, the dulcimer is a modal instrument. Yet when I first confronted the concept of a <u>mode</u> I found it quite confusing; it seemed as if there were as many modes as I had toes. Later I discovered I was wrong: in reality there are more modes than my ten toes. Nevertheless, in time I have managed to get a few of the fourteen modes (seven standard and seven "new"*) under control, or under foot you might say, and now I switch easily through four of the more common modes. Much can be said about these modes which have been handed down to us from the ancient Greeks, but for our purposes let us think of a mode as being basically: 1.) a seven note octave (verses a chromatic twelve tone octave); and 2.) a pre-established arrangement or alignment between the strings on your dulcimer (a set mathematical progression across the strings). Each mode has its own peculiar string arrangement and sound, and consequently utilizes different fingering positions to make up the same chords. (See the chord charts in the back of this book.) <u>You can tune your dulcimer in any key in any of the modes you wish</u>, though practically speaking you will find that your string gauges will limit you to a five or six key range before they either break or buzz from slackness. It is of great importance that you understand that within a mode tuned in one key you can also play songs written in other keys. This is called <u>cross-keying</u>. For instance, out of the Mixolydian mode key of D (my favorite tuning), I am also able to play songs in the relative keys of: G, A, Em, Bm, and partially in the keys of: Am, F♯m, and C. I accomplish this simply by playing the notes found in the corresponding scales of these keys, and the chords used in these keys (often accomplished by using my third or little finger to make barre chords, so creating a moveable capo-like effect.) For further examples, out of the Mixolydian key of C, you can play in the relative keys of: F, G, Am, Dm; out of the Mix. key of E, in the relative keys of: A, B, C♯m, F♯m.

Since a majority of the tunes in this book are written for the Mixolydian mode, we will use this as our base mode from which to approach the three other modes employed in this book.

* The difference being that the bass and middle strings reverse positions; i.e. the bass note switches to the middle string, and vice-versa.

The Mixolydian Mode: A major mode, associated with the sun (and so with lightness) by the Greeks, having the distinctive characteristic of a flattened seventh. (In the key of C in a diatonic major scale you find the notes: C,D,E,F,G,A,B,C; while in the Mixolydian mode you have: C,D,E,F,G,A,B♭,C.) A large number of old pipe and fiddle tunes are written in this mode, and I find that the octave split between the melody (or first) string and the bass string with a fifth tone in the middle makes this a more flexible mode than the Ionian (the other major mode). You can walk the melody line across the strings, as well as up and down.

Tuning: Select your keytone (the note corresponding to the key you wish to tune to) and tune your first string to this note.*Next, fret the middle string at the third fret and tune it till you have the same tone as the first string played open. Finally, fret the bass string at the seventh (octave) fret and tune till you have the same tone as the first string played open or the middle string fretted at the third. Here are the notes you would then have on your dulcimer if you were in one of these three keys. (Remember there are nine other possible keys, one for every note in the chromatic scale, and that the basic arrangement will always remain the same - in terms of the piano, a 1-5-7 progression, seven being the octave point.)

Mixolydian Mode: 1st or Melody	Middle	Bass	Key
DD	A	D	(D)
CC	G	C	(C)
EE	B	E	(E)
(1)	(5)	(7)	

The New Ionian Mode: A major mode, with a completely major scale (C,D,E,F,G,A,B,C). I find the New Ionian mode more flexible than the Standard Ionian, and exceedingly simple to slip into from the Mixolydian mode.

Tuning: All you do is drop the middle string one full step; such that you fret it at the fourth fret now instead of at the third to get the same tone as the first string played open. The melody or first string and the bass string remain exactly the same as they were in the Mixolydian mode.

* Buy yourself a small pitch-pipe or a tuning fork, or tune to another instrument. Practice and careful listening will make tuning easier. Generally it is easier to hear two notes come together if you will tune up rather than tuning down to meet the chosen note.

New Ionian Mode:

Melody	Middle	Bass	Key
DD	G	D	(G)
CC	F	C	(F)
EE	A	E	(A)
(1)	(4)	(7)	

Many of the chord patterns used in the Mixolydian mode are used in the New Ionian though the same fingerings assume new chord names.

Standard Ionian:

Melody	Middle	Bass	Key
DD	D	G	(G)
CC	C	F	(F)
EE	E	A	(A)
(1)	(1)	(4)	

(Here the melody and middle strings share the same note, while the bass string is fretted at the fourth to give the same tone as any of the first three strings open. Note however that we do not have the octave difference between the melody and the middle strings here that we find existing between the melody and the bass strings in the New Ionian.)

The Aeolian Mode: A minor mode, having the normal minor scale (C,D,E♭,F,G,A♭,B♭, C). To tune into the Aeolian from the Mixolydian we have a choice. Either we can lower the melody strings one full step (leaving the middle and bass strings exactly as they were), or we can raise the middle and bass strings one full step or note (leaving the melody strings as they were).

Tuning: In either case we begin by fretting the melody string at the first fret and the middle string at the third fret. Holding these strings fretted simultaneously we can now raise the middle string to the same tone as that of the melody string, or we can lower the melody string to the tone of the middle string. Finally, we adjust the bass string so that it has the same tone as the melody and the middle strings fretted at the first and third frets respectively (i.e. we don't have to move our fingers from their original position.) If you lowered the melody string one step the bass string remains where it was (you don't have to retune it); if you raised the middle string one step leaving the first string alone, then you will also raise the bass string one full step.

Aeolian Mode:	Melody	Middle	Bass	Key
	CC	A	D	(Dm)
	DD	B	E	(Em)
	B♭ B♭	G	C	(Cm)
	(1)	(6)	(8)	

(The Aeolian mode is a hauntingly beautiful mode particularly lovely for Renaissance tunes like <u>Greensleeves</u> or <u>Lord Lovel</u>. It may sound way out of tune for a while to your ears, but give it a chance.)

<u>The New Dorian Mode</u>: Called the mountain minor, this mode has an irregular minor scale (C,D,E♭,F,G,A,B♭,C). Considered the "Bestower of Wisdom and Clarity" this mode occurs frequently in traditional British and American folk music.

<u>Tuning</u>: In relation to the Mixolydian Mode only the bass string is raised one full step (the melody and middle strings remain unchanged). Fret the melody string at the first fret and raise the bass string one step to this same note. From the Aeolian mode, lower the middle string one full step (the bass and melody strings remaining unchanged). To do this fret the middle string at the third fret and lower it to the same tone as the melody string struck open.

New Dorian Mode:	Melody	Middle	Bass	Key
	DD	A	E	(Am)
	CC	G	D	(Gm)
	EE	B	F♯	(Bm)
	(1)	(5)	(8)	
Standard Dorian:				
	DD	E	A	(Am)
	CC	D	G	(Gm)
	GG	A	D	(Dm)
	(1)	(2)	(5)	

There are three other modes though they will play no part in this book. They are the <u>Lydian</u> Mode (ex: DD-G-C= key of C); the <u>Locrian</u> Mode (ex: B♭ B♭-A-D= key of D); and the <u>Phrygian</u> Mode (ex: E♭ E♭-G-C= key of Cm).

Review: A mode is a seven tone, pre-ordained arrangement between the strings on your dulcimer. It can also be thought of as a pre-established series of whole and half steps among the seven notes which make up the scale of the key in the mode you are tuned in. Or as Neal Hellman words it, "A mode is a sequence of tones and semitones within a musical scale. Each mode has its own combination of tones and semitones (steps and $\frac{1}{2}$ steps)."

In a chromatic scale we have 12 notes with a $\frac{1}{2}$ step between each note.

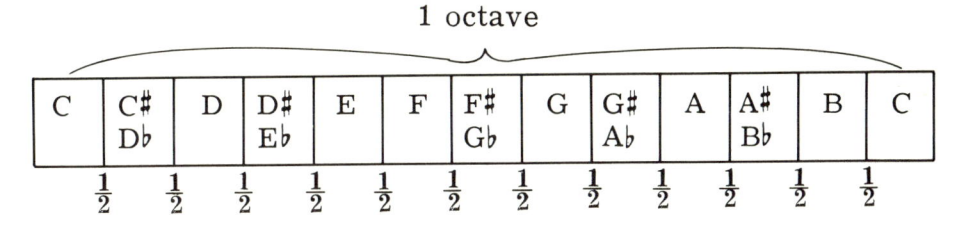

1 octave

C	C#/Db	D	D#/Eb	E	F	F#/Gb	G	G#/Ab	A	A#/Bb	B	C
$\frac{1}{2}$	$\frac{1}{2}$	$\frac{1}{2}$	$\frac{1}{2}$	$\frac{1}{2}$	$\frac{1}{2}$	$\frac{1}{2}$	$\frac{1}{2}$	$\frac{1}{2}$	$\frac{1}{2}$	$\frac{1}{2}$	$\frac{1}{2}$	

In a modal scale the series of half and whole steps varies: (Key of C)

Mixolydian Mode: 1 1 $\frac{1}{2}$ 1 1 $\frac{1}{2}$ 1 = C D E F G A Bb C
                                                                  1 1 $\frac{1}{2}$ 1 1 $\frac{1}{2}$ 1

New Ionian: 1 1 $\frac{1}{2}$ 1 1 1 $\frac{1}{2}$ = C D E F G A B C

New Dorian: 1 $\frac{1}{2}$ 1 1 1 $\frac{1}{2}$ 1 = C D Eb F G A Bb C

Aeolian: 1 $\frac{1}{2}$ 1 1 $\frac{1}{2}$ 1 1 = C D Eb F G Ab Bb C

Note: I do not find this step- $\frac{1}{2}$ step method of visualizing a mode to be of particular help, but perhaps you will find it of some assistance. Generally speaking, the more you use the modes and their various tunings the more you will come to understand the subtle complexities of your dulcimer.

Perhaps this would be the best time to lay out the dulcimer's fret board schemata before moving on. Starting at the 3rd fret the 'standard' dulcimer fingerboard is arranged in a <u>diatonic</u> progression: whole step - whole step - half step - whole step - whole step - whole step - half.

Diatonic steps: 1 1 $\frac{1}{2}$ 1 1 1 $\frac{1}{2}$

		E	F#	G	A	B	C	C#/D	E	F#	G
BASS	D										
		B	C#	D	E	F#	G	G#/A	B	C#	D
MIDDLE	A										
		E	F#	G	A	B	C	C#/D	E	F#	G
MELODY	D										
FRET:		0	1	2	3	4	5	6 6½ 7	8	9	10

It should be duly noted that the $6\frac{1}{2}$ fret is a modern addition to the modal dulcimer. An important one I think since it allows us to play in a major (diatonic) as well as a modal scale, from the open position (D to D), and is also a fundamental factor in cross-keying. Many modern dulcimers have the $6\frac{1}{2}$ fret built into them, but if your dulcimer does not have this extra half step it can be easily added by any good instrument maker or repairman.

A WORD ABOUT STRING GAUGES

Since I play out of the Mixolydian mode I prefer to have a pronounced distinction between the tone of my melody and middle strings. Through trial and error I have found the following gauges give my dulcimer its optimum sound:

    Melody or First Strings: two .10 (ten) gauge strings

    Middle: one .14 or .15 gauge string

    Bass: one .22 gauge wound string (phosphor—bronze if available)

If your dulcimer takes <u>loop-end</u> strings ask for banjo strings from the singles bin; if your instrument requires <u>ball-end</u> strings ask for guitar singles in these same gauges. Should you find you desire a deeper more bassey tone, increase the gauge size till you discover the optimum set for your instrument. Another common set of dulcimer strings made up for those who prefer to play out of the Standard Ionian mode would be: two .12's on the melody course, a third .12 on the middle, and a .21 gauge wound string on the bass.

HOW TO READ THE NUMERICAL TABLATURE IN THIS BOOK

The numerical tabs contained within this book are written for a traditional three course mountain dulcimer. The three lines of tablature staff found below the musical score of each song relate directly to the strings of your dulcimer as they appear when you are playing your instrument. <u>Reading vertically down</u>, the top number applies to the corresponding fret position located on the bass string, the middle number to the middle string, the bottom number to the melody string.

```
BASS COURSE    T _____ 2 _____
                                                       ⎫
MIDDLE         A _____ 3 _____ ⎬ = D chord in the
                                                       ⎪   Mixolydian mode
MELODY         B _____ 4 _____ ⎭   Key of D
```

The numbers themselves relate directly to the corresponding fret found on the dulcimer fretboard, pictured as follows:

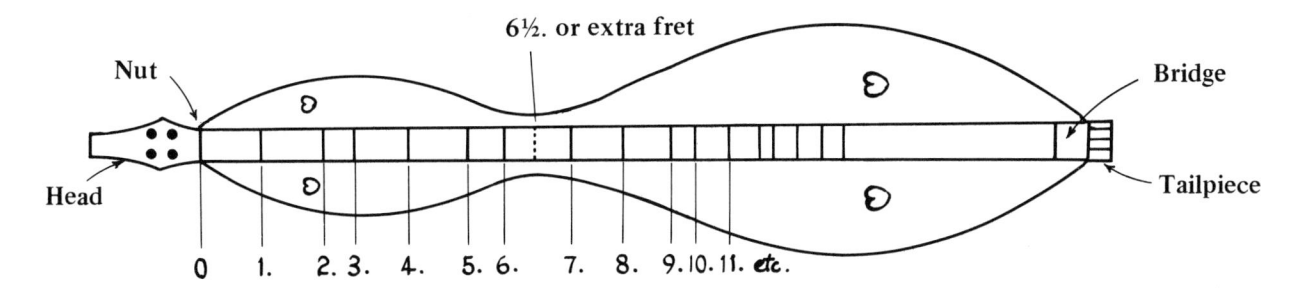

To play the tab as indicated, push down the appropriate string just to the left of the indicated fret. When you see a zero (0) this means the string is to be played open, an x in the tab means the string is not to be played. In this book if a series of melody line notes share the same tab, that tab will be given only for the first note in the series and should be held in this same position until a new tab is presented. What I have tried to do throughout is to put the appropriate chord (or piece of that chord) behind the melody line note. Therefore I give you the chord, the melody line notes, and the fingering I use to give the song a fuller sound by putting the chord and melody line together. By all means construct your own arrangements, using partial chords, or different fingerings for the indicated chords - play the songs as you hear them, make them yours.°

For some few songs I have indicated alternative arrangements using tablature only. The time signature of the melody line is indicated below the numerical tab by a series of whole, half, quarter, eighth, and sixteenth notes indicating how long each note is to be held. For example, let's look at the first three bars of The Touchstone (p.58):

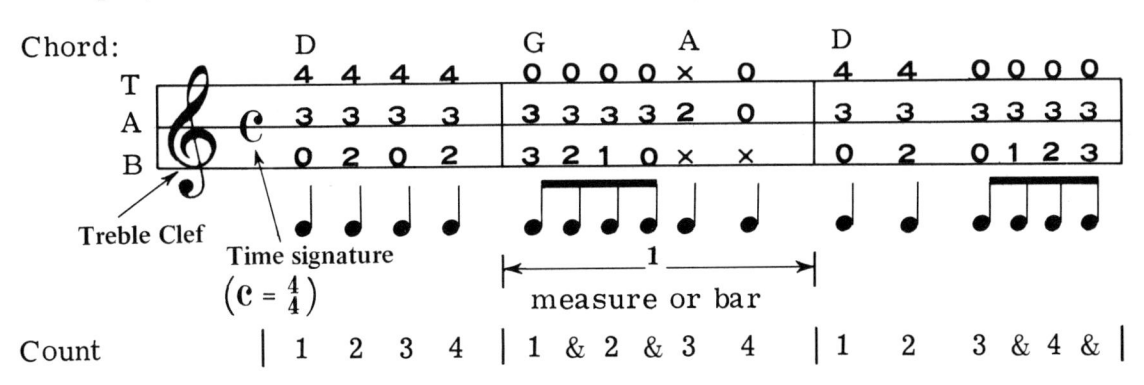

°You should note that if you are unable to play full three finger chords you can always play the bottom (melody string) number and add extra strings when and if you wish. Just follow the melody line and play the middle and bass strings as open drones.

PLACING CHORDS BEHIND THE MELODY LINE

This venerable technique has long been used by all sorts of string players. I find it particularly helpful and appealing when playing solo since it provides a fuller richer sound, supplying rhythm and lead at the same time. This style may seem formidable at first, but as with any new challenge, in time it will grow to be more familiar than formidable as your fingers loosen up and the basic chord structures become second nature.

Learning the melody line should remain your first step when approaching a new song. (Let me reiterate, I'm speaking about my basic method; by all means take what you find useful and incorporate it into your own approach.) Working with the melody line will help you realize early on whether or not you want to invest your time and effort in the song. More importantly, you will begin to work on the guts of the song, its timing and phrasing. This will also give you some idea of which specific chord positions you will later use; it should also give you an inkling of when you may wish to resort to an unadorned melody line to see you through a particularly intricate run or a long jump between two notes.

When you have the song's basic timing and melody under control (which does not necessarily mean memorized) you can start adding the underlying chord structure. Before we begin to discuss full chords or partial chords, we should note that there are several ways you can embellish a song played out of the Mixolydian mode. And anyone can use these techniques almost immediately. Let's look at a song everyone knows, Oh Susanna by Stephen Foster ("Oh, I come from Alabama with a dulcimer on my knees"), and see how to use two basic chordal techniques: namely the octave split, and set chords. Once again we learn the melody line first.

Mixolydian mode
Key of D

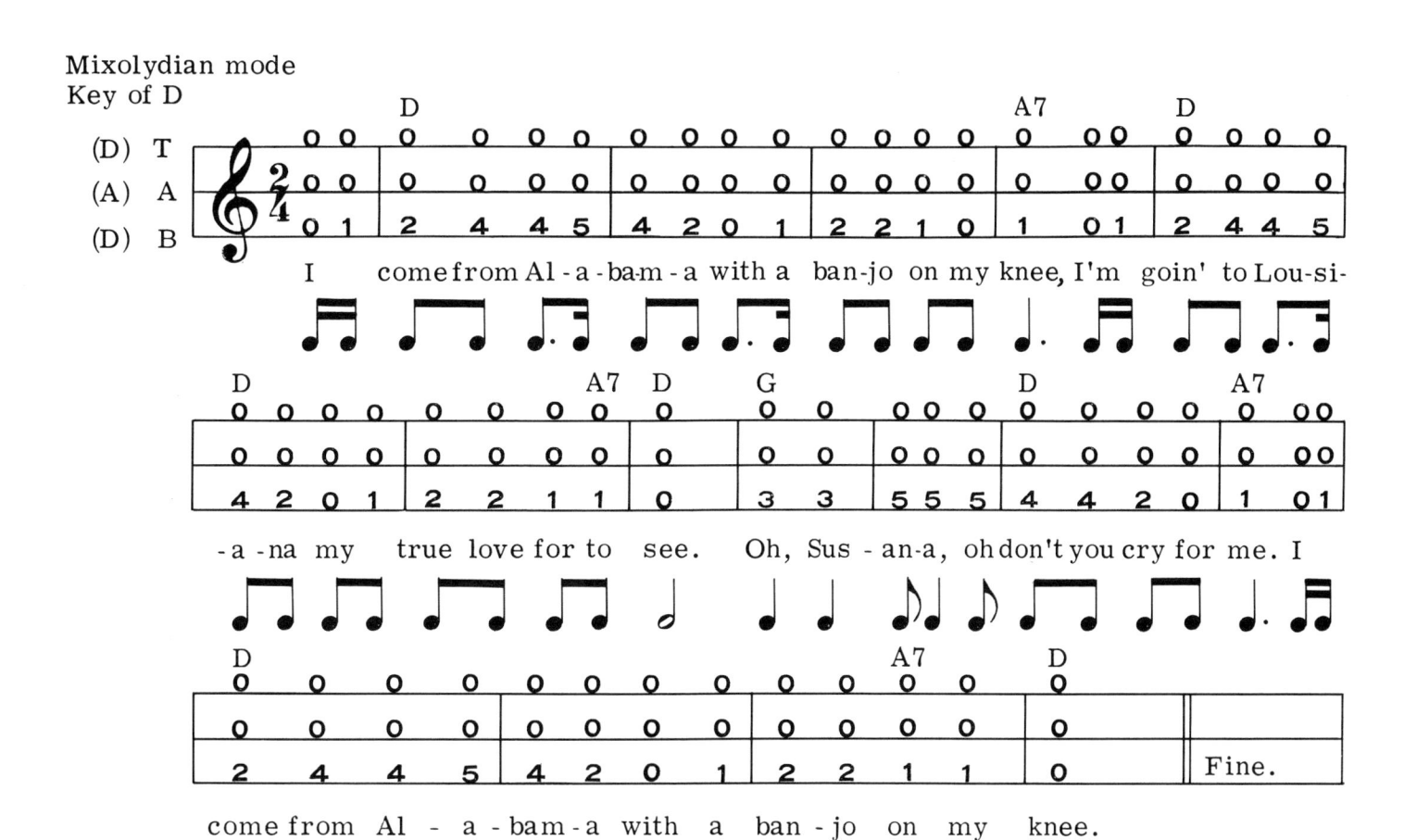

[Tablature with lyrics:]

I come from Al-a-bam-a with a ban-jo on my knee, I'm goin' to Lou-si-

-a-na my true love for to see. Oh, Sus-an-a, oh don't you cry for me. I

come from Al-a-bam-a with a ban-jo on my knee. Fine.

This is the basic melody line played on the first or melody string alone, using the middle and bass strings to provide a constant droning D chord (the open strings being the notes <u>A</u> and <u>D</u> respectively, two thirds of a full D chord which is made up of the notes D, A, and F♯). To use the <u>octave split</u> all you have to do is reach across and exactly duplicate on the bass string what you are doing on the melody string (I use my index finger on the melody, my second finger on the bass string). The TAB now looks like this:

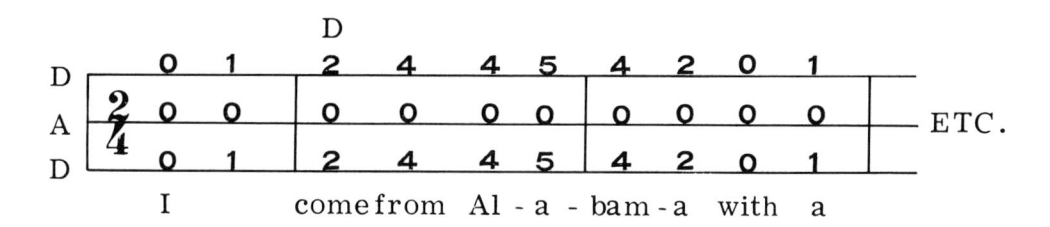

[Tablature example with lyrics: I come from Al-a-bam-a with a] ETC.

To use the <u>set chord</u> device place your second finger on the third fret of the middle string and leave it there for the entire song moving the melody line around this pivot point. The TAB now reads:

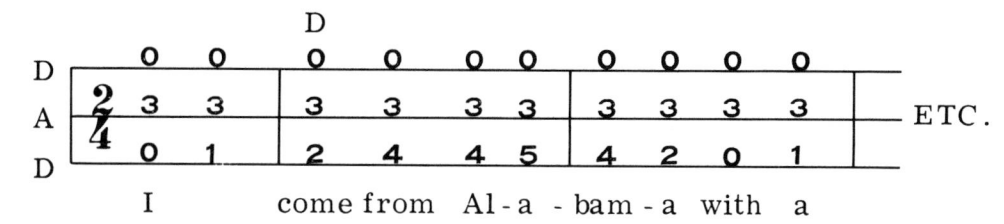

[Tablature example with lyrics: I come from Al-a-bam-a with a] ETC.

There seem to be several key points along the fret-board which work as primary set chord positions on the middle string; these nodes being: the 3rd, 4th, 7th, and 10th frets. Pivoting the melody line around these set points will dramatically alter the droning quality of your dulcimer, and get you started well down the road of partial chords.*

Partial chords are created when you use two fingers to hold down two notes on two distinct strings thereby completing part of a full chord normally comprised of three or four notes. For instance, if a D chord looks like this:

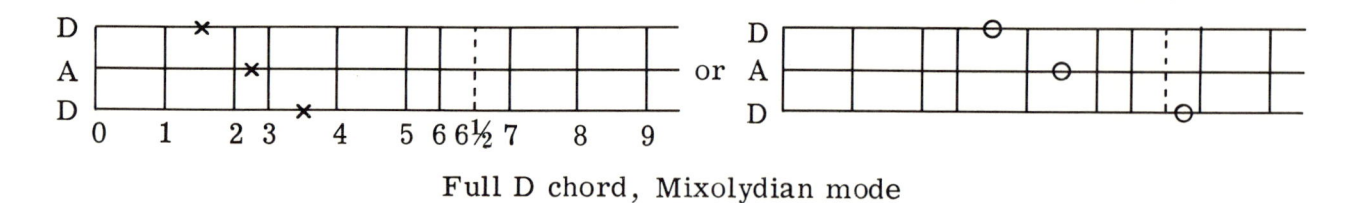

Full D chord, Mixolydian mode

A partial D chord could look like:

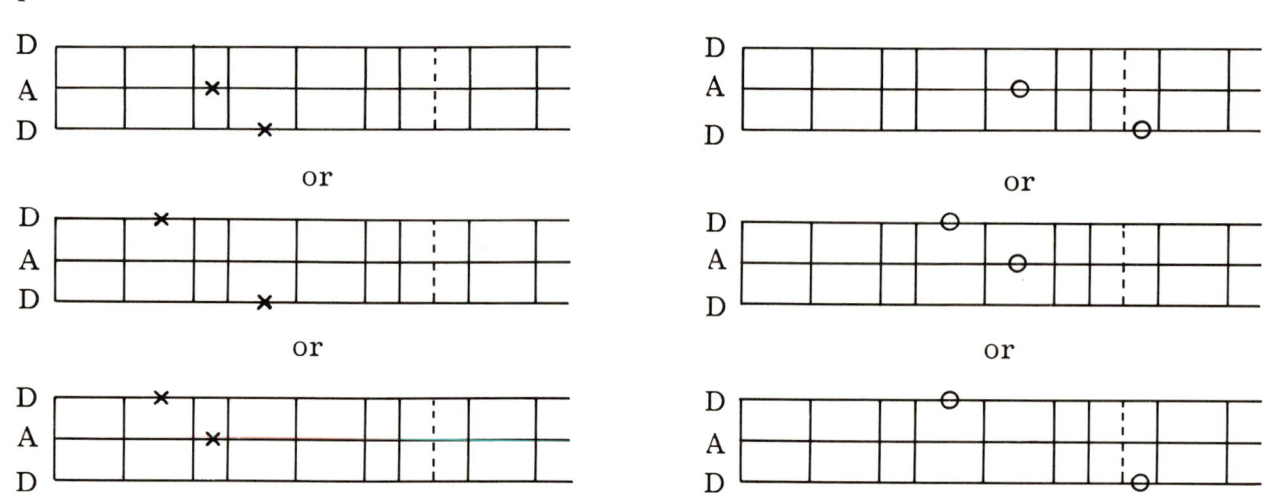

So you have a vast number of possibilities to choose from (and it should be stated here that <u>in the Mixolydian mode you can invert</u>, or switch finger positions on bass and melody strings, <u>for all chords</u>). Partial chords are usually quicker to use than full three finger chords, and at the very least will start you out towards full chord use.

* By mixing up the order with which you use <u>set chords</u>, <u>octave splits</u>, and the straightforward melody line you can make a very simple song sound quite nicely embellished. Remember that everything you do in the first octave range (frets 0-7) can be repeated exactly, one octave higher (frets 7-14).

16

The idea behind partial chords and <u>full chords</u> is exactly the same: namely, to take the melody line, read the chords found above the line, and then use the appropriate notes from those chords behind the melody note. Look back at the chorus from <u>Oh Susanna</u>, ("Oh, Susanna, oh don't you cry for me.") We will need to find the chord structures for G, D, and A7, so turn to the chord charts in the back of the book and look them up in the Mixolydian section. Knowing where the notes of the melody line fall, these three chord positions seem best suited.

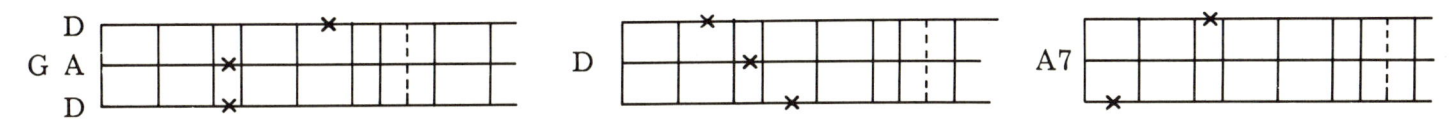

```
    D                              ×                          ×
G A      ×              D     ×                    A7
    D        ×                         ×                ×
```

When we put the full chord behind the melody line the TAB now reads:

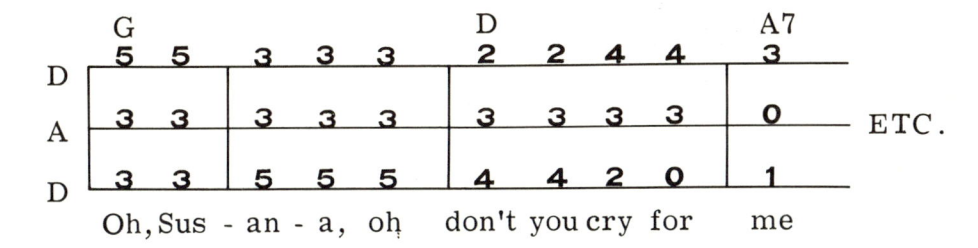

```
        G                       D              A7
        5  5   3  3  3   2   2  4  4    3
   D
   A    3  3   3  3  3   3   3  3  3    0    ─── ETC.
   D    3  3   5  5  5   4   4  2  0    1
       Oh, Sus-an-a, oh  don't you cry for  me
```

So you have the basic proceedure: 1.) learn the melody line; 2.) consult the chord charts to determine which chord position best lends itself, both to where the melody line is and will be next; and 3.) finally figure out which fingers to use so that you don't trip the light fantastic all over yourself and your song.

17

BARRE CHORDING WITH YOUR LITTLE FINGER

Since I do not use my thumb when playing the dulcimer I have learned to compensate for the loss of this fifth digit by making extensive use of the technique known as <u>barre chording</u>. Barre chords are formed when you stop (hold down) all the strings across one fret using only one finger. A guitarist uses his index finger to form barre chords because his hand is held behind the neck and fretboard of his instrument. When playing a dulcimer however, your hand is positioned over the fretboard, palm down, fingers pointing out and away. Consequently the little finger assumes the function of forming barre chords. At first barreing with my little finger was both difficult and painful; the finger seemed to have a will of its own, deciding when and where to go, while the strings cut into it and the outside muscle of my hand slowly cramped up. Familiar stories to anyone who has ever learned to barre chord a stringed instrument. In time however, you gain control, subtlety, and quickness with the little finger, a callous develops to shield your tender digit, and you sport the hottest 'adductor' muscle on the beach. And most importantly your dulcimer playing will have improved dramatically. Even if you use your thumb (and I suspect you do), the ability to form barre chords will prove most useful for a number of reasons.

Being able to barre with your little finger provides you with a built in moveable capo by which you may change keys within a mode; barreing at the correct fret in effect 'retunes' the dulcimer. In the Mixolydian mode key of D you can produce these capoed keys:

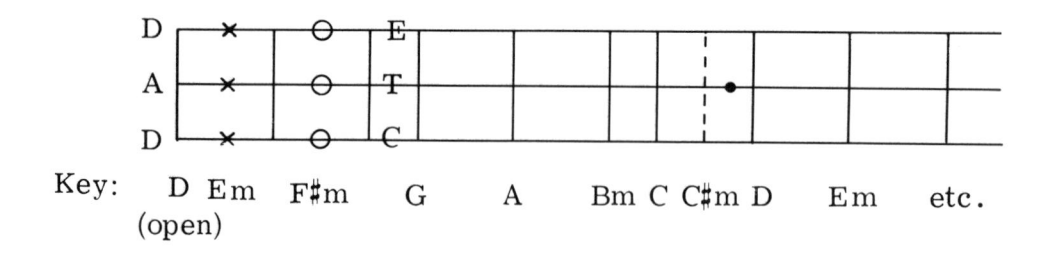

```
D |--x--|--o--|E    |     |     |     |  .  |     |     |
A |--x--|--o--|T    |     |     |     |  •  |     |     |
D |--x--|--o--|C    |     |     |     |  .  |     |     |
```

Key: D Em F♯m   G   A   Bm C C♯m D   Em   etc.
(open)

(You should remember that besides capoing, it is necessary to play the correct notes within a key. To figure out these notes is simple enough since the formula always remains the same: full step, full, half, full, full, full, half step back to the octave for a major scale. Remember there is a half step between each note in the chromatic scale: C, C♯, D, D♯, E, F, F♯, G, G♯, A, A♯, B, C.)

Using your little finger in the barre position will enable you to slide from one chord into any other sharing one or more notes in the bottom fret position. For example, in the key of D Mixolydian mode:

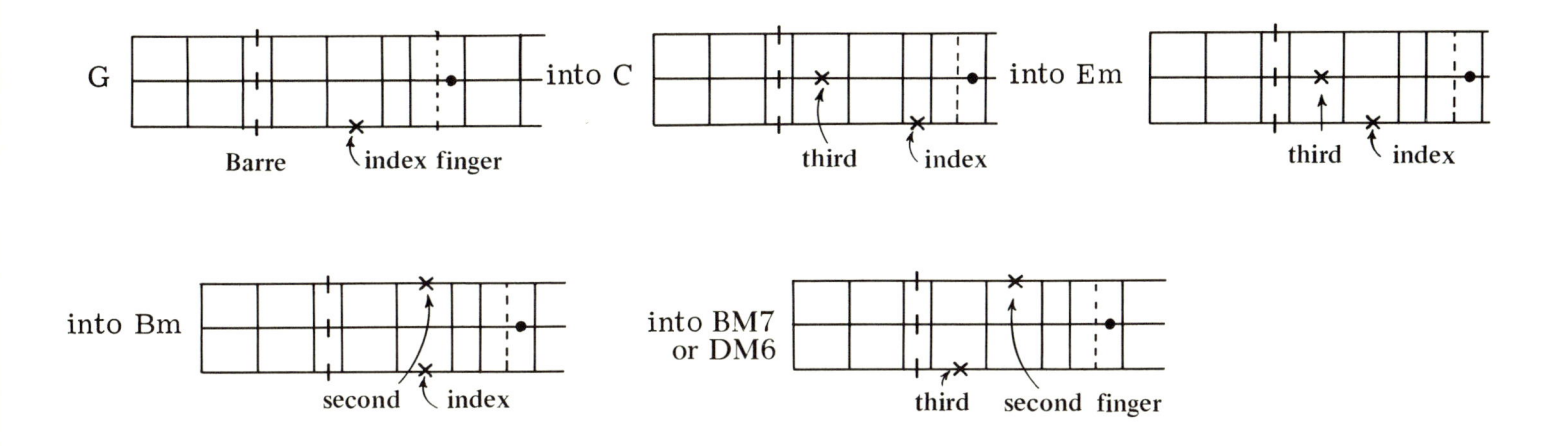

In the Mixolydian mode or the New Ionian mode, the barre position allows you to invert chords quickly and easily since the bass and melody strings share the same note one octave apart.

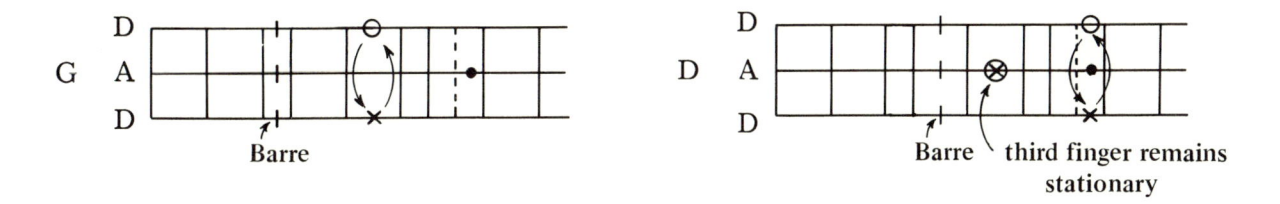

I find the barre chord to be of great help and make extensive use of it throughout my arrangements.

SECTION #1

Songs from
"NOT LICKED YET"*

*Solo dulcimer album recorded in 1981 on the Centennial Label (CCR-1981). Available from M. Biggs/R.R. #3 Box 367B/Galena, Mo. 65656.

Photo by Max Tyndall

PEPPERMINT STICK RAG

Mixolydian D
(DD A D)

by Mark Biggs

This song should swing along in a red and white swirl, with a heavy driving syncopation.

Photo by Mark Biggs

TOMORROW TODAY

Mixolydian D
(DD A D)

If you can get two dulcimers going this song sounds real nice with one playing part A while the other plays part B.

by Mark Biggs

Sequence A B A B A

Mixolydian D
(DD A D)

SONYA'S SONG

Written for my neice, Sonya Mun, this tune starts slow and builds steam all the way to the end. Don't let all the notes in the score scare you; they are there simply to give you some concrete idea of the constantly changing syncopation which gives the song its character. Actually there are four basic parts or phrases that change form through tempo; learn these four phrases and the song is a snap.

by Mark Biggs

A
D A7 D G D Em7 G D
G D Em7 G D G D Em7 G D
B
D G A G D A7 D
C
G Em7 G D G Em7 G D
G Em7 G D G Em7 D
B
D G A G D A7 D
D
D G D A7 D G D D A7 D
D G A G A G D A7 G D A7 D D G A G A G D A7 G D A7 D
B
D G A G D A7
C
G

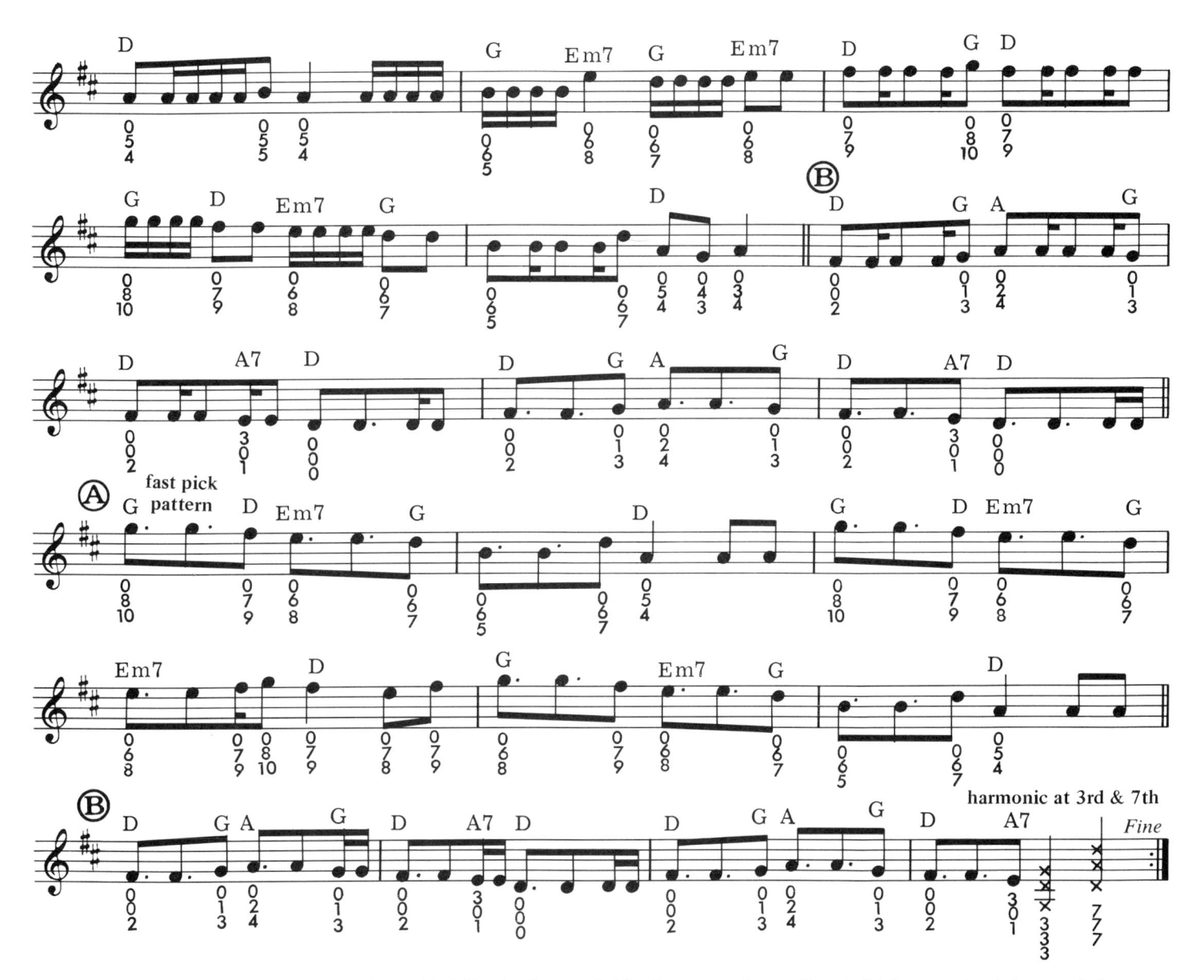

Though each segment varies slightly in form & timing, perhaps it might be easiest to envision 'Sonya's Song' as the following sequence: A B C B/A B C B/D B C B/A B

Photo by Max Tyndall

WILDWOOD FLOWER

Mixolydian D
(DD A D)

I play this one with a spirited tempo, though it's sweet as a slow lament as well. Almost everybody and their grandmother knows and asks for this classic folk song.

Trad. American Folk Song

Photo by Mark Biggs

OLD JOE CLARK

Mixolydian D
(DD A D)

Old Joe Clark is a hot toe tapper with a million verses. I've given you only a few, so feel free to make up more. I have a feeling that's what people have been doing for years. You can play this 8va (one octave higher) also, starting at the eleventh fret.

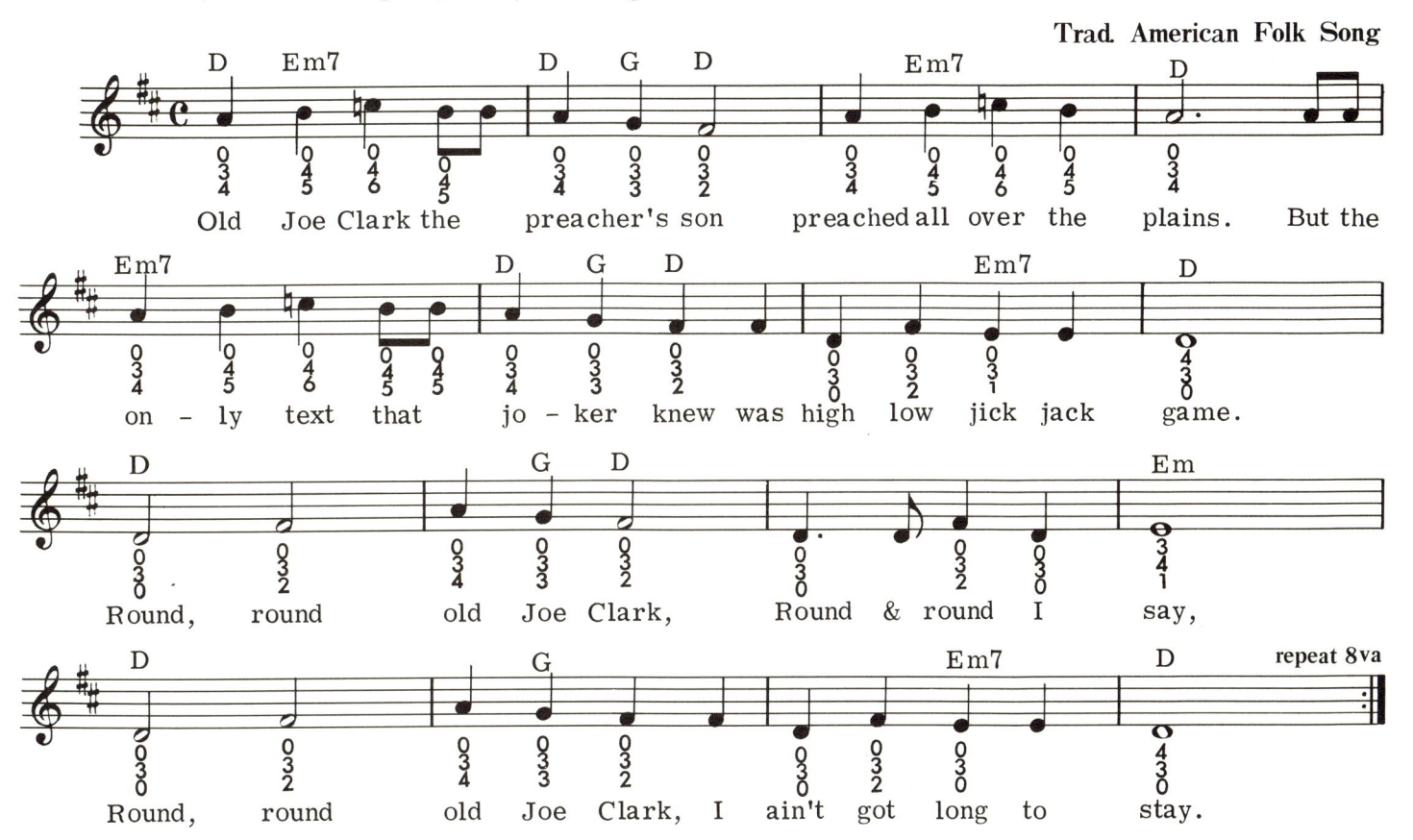

Trad. American Folk Song

Old Joe Clark the preacher's son preached all over the plains. But the on-ly text that jo-ker knew was high low jick jack game. Round, round old Joe Clark, Round & round I say, Round, round old Joe Clark, I ain't got long to stay.

I used to live on a mountain top,
Now I live in town.
I'm staying at the big hotel
Just a courtin' Betsy Brown.

Singing fare you well, old Joe Clark,
Good-bye Betsy Brown.
Fare you well, old Joe Clark
I'm about to leave this town.

I went down to old Joe's place,
Old Joe wasn't home.
So I jumped in bed with old Joe's wife,
And broke her tucking comb.

Fare thee well, old Joe Clark,
Fare thee well I say.
Fare thee well, old Joe Clark
I'm going far away.

Now I won't go to old Joe's house,
Tell you the reason why.
I can't get around his garden patch
For tearing down all his rye.

Singing oh no old Joe Clark,
Tell you the reason why,
Singing oh no I won't go,
I won't see that guy.

I won't go to old Joe's place.
I told you that here before.
Cause once he fed me in an old hog trough
And I won't go there no more.

Singing round round old Joe Clark,
Round and round I say,
Why he'd foller me ten thousand miles
Just to hear my dulcimer play.

NOBODY HOME

Mixolydian D
(DD A D)

If you live in the Ozarks very long, you learn to use Ma Bell before going over to your neighbor's house unannounced. You tend to get a little peeved at yourself if you make that half hour drive only to find nobody around. And naturally if you do such a foolhardy thing, when you get back home the phone will be ringing and of course if will be those selfsame friends saying "Come on over." This full tilt boogie is just my way of saying, "It's a long way to go to find nobody home."

by Mark Biggs

(A) Full tilt boogie

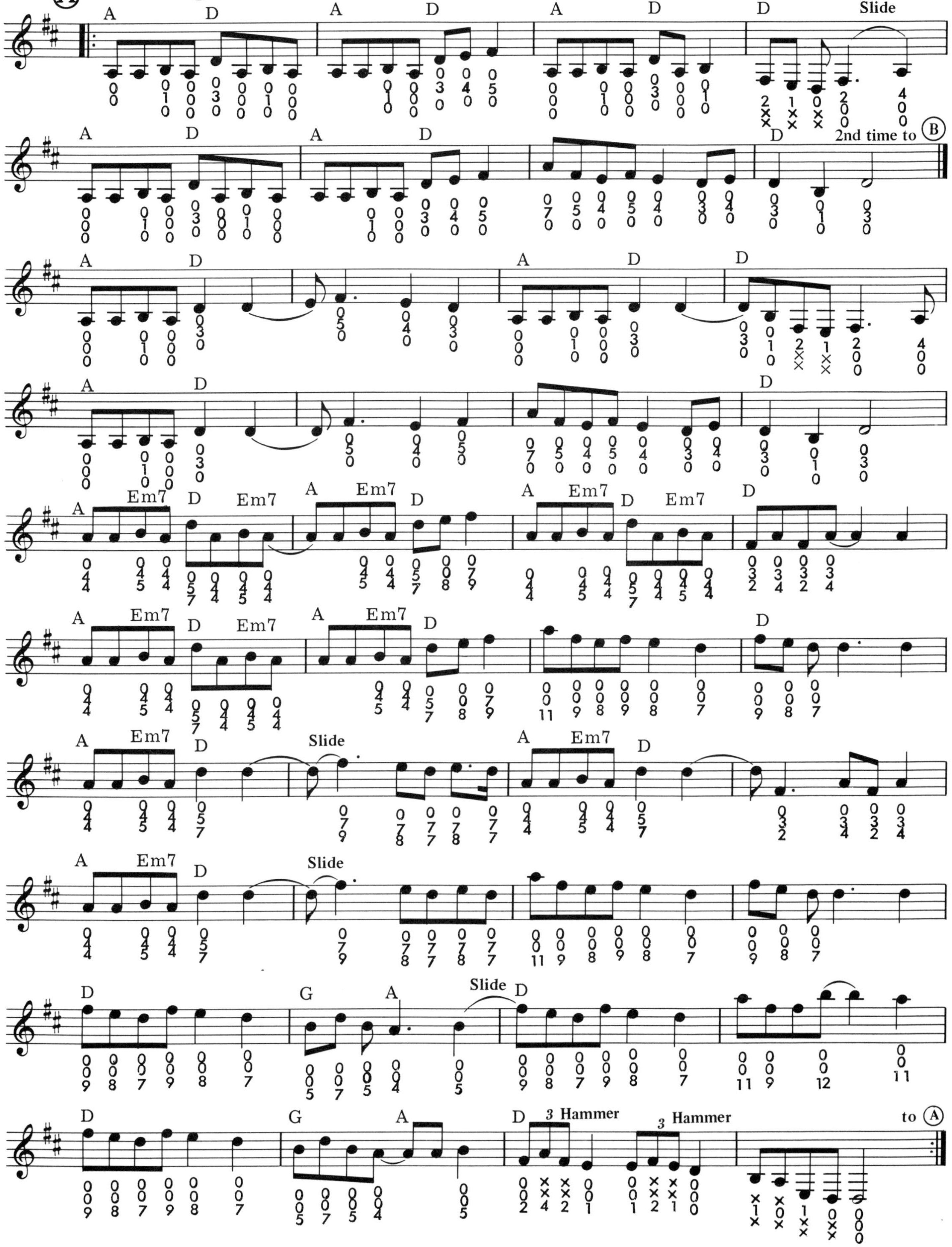

B
Slide
Hammer
(repeat preceeding 2 bars again)
Bend the note
Fine

Photo by Max Tyndall

THE PARTING GLASS

Mixolydian D
(DD A D)

Play this lovely air with all the emotion of a leave-taking from dear friends.

With warm emotion

Trad. Irish Air

8va (one octave higher)

I play through this peice once low, once high, & end on the third time through on the low part.

New Ionian G
(DD G D)

THE WINTER'S LAMENT TO SPRING
(& SPRING'S REPLY)

Composed on both sides of the Atlantic, Winter in England and Spring in the Ozarks, this song was undoubtedly influenced by a summer's worth of listening to Vivaldi's <u>Four Seasons</u>. It speaks to me of life's cycles: of death and rebirth, the refrains of the old becoming the new and the new becoming the old even as it mocks and mimics its future past. It is the cracking and carping of the ice on the pond under a March sun - a song of lamentation transformed into a joyous chant of rejuvenation.

by Mark Biggs

C D C G D7 G
D Lively tempo
Em G D G C G D G
Em G D G Em G F 3 D7
G Em G C G D G
G Em G C G D G
Am G D Am
G Bm Am G D
C D C Em D C D
A
C D7 G Dm G Dm Dm7 G D
Dm G Dm G D G D

Perhaps it would be easiest to envision this song as the following sequence: A B A C D C A B A

Photo by Mark Biggs

FAREWELL AND ADIEU YE FINE SPANISH LADIES

Aeolian Em
(DD B E)
Key of Bm

This lovely old song seems simultaneously happy to be sailing away and sad to be leaving - a sense of sweet remorse you might say. When I play this piece I hear these words:

> Farewell & adieu all ye fine Spanish ladies,
> Farewell and adieu for we sail o'er the ocean.
> Though we may not meet once again,
> Yet I say that I love you,
> All you fine Spanish ladies, all dressed in black lace.

17th Cent. English Sea Chantey

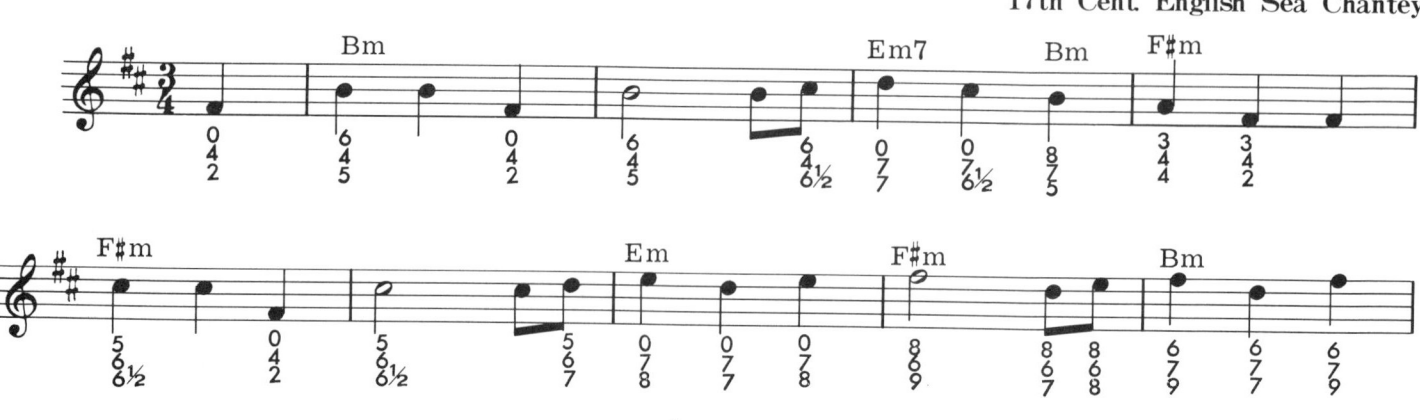

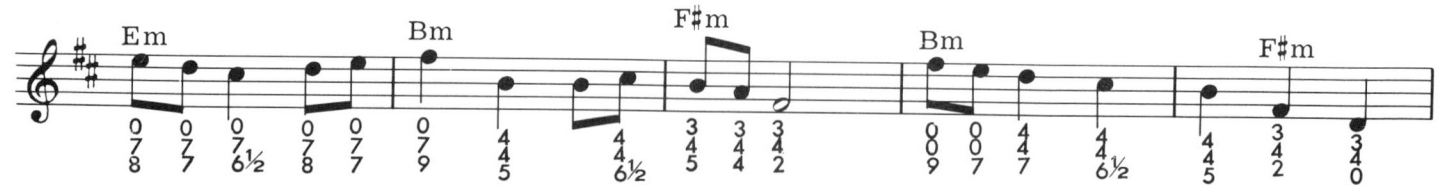

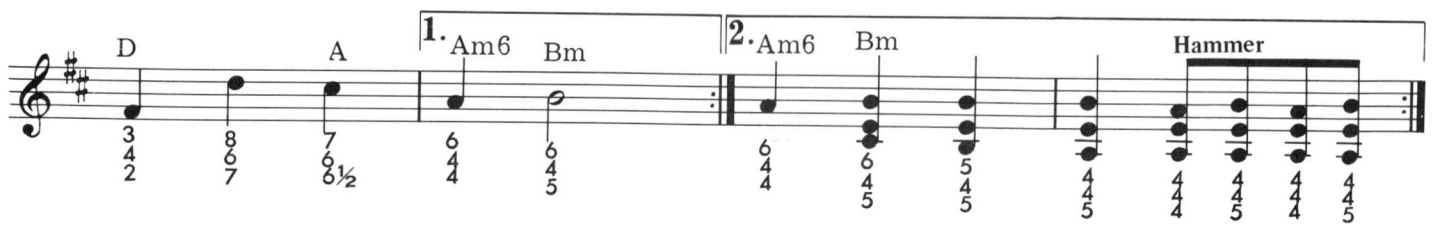

Photo by Mark Biggs

Mixolydian D
(DD A D)

THE ASHGROVE

A very well known Welsh folksong which I play up-tempo not having been aware originally that an ashgrove in medieval times was a graveyard. So the song continues to carry for me the mental image of yellow ash leaves blowing about under a warm autumn sun.

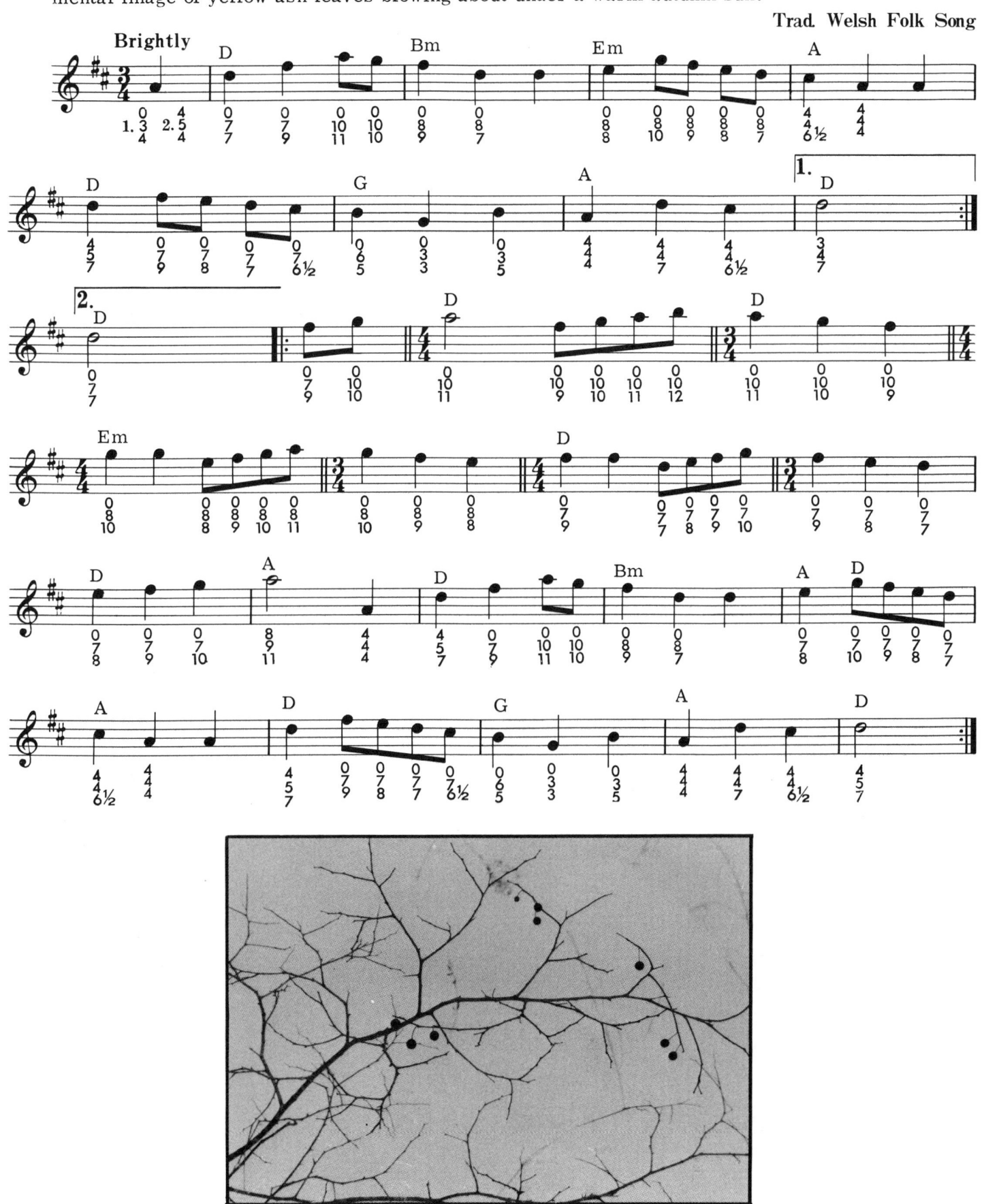

Trad. Welsh Folk Song

Photo by Mark Biggs

SOLDIER'S JOY

Mixolydian D
(DD A D)

One of best known most often played fiddle tunes, played with the jaunty expression of a soldier's joy come payday.

Trad. English Folk Song

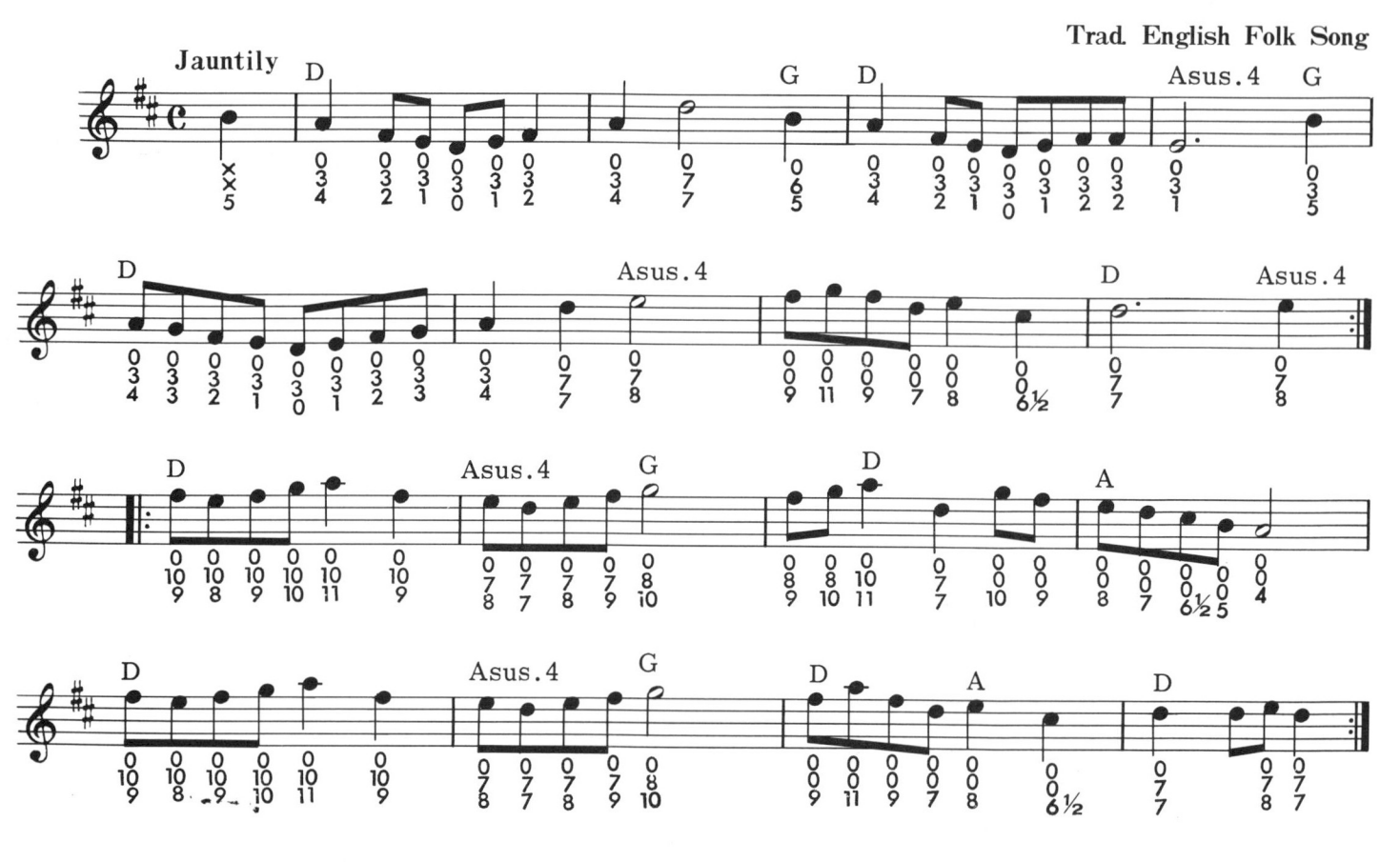

Photo by Mark Biggs

GREENSLEEVES

Aeolian Dm
(CC A D)

One of the oldest standards, dating back pre-1600.

Trad. English

LORD LOVEL

Aeolian Dm
(CC A D)

17th Cent. Trad. English

DRILL YE TARRIER'S, DRILL

Aeolian Dm
(CC A D)

The tarriers were the men who went in front of the track laying crews to prepare the roadbed for the rails to come. They were traditionally Irish, most often first generation immigrants, and inevitably over-worked and underpaid, or so their song goes. Play it with a steady pile-driving tempo.

Trad. American Work Song

It was early in the morning at seven o'-clock There's twenty tarriers out drilling on the rocks, When the boss comes along, and he says keep still and come down heavy on them cast iron drills, And drill ye tarrier's, drill. Drill ye tarrier's, drill. Though you work all day for the sugar in your tay, down behind the rail-way, Still drill ye tarr-i-ers drill and blast and fire.

Now the boss was a fine man down to the ground,
And he married a lady six feet round;
Well she baked good bread, and she baked it well,
But she baked it hard as the holes of hell! So...

Well the new foreman was Jean McCann;
By God, he was a blamed mean cuss of a man.
When last week a premature blast went off,
A mile in the air went big Jim Goff, still...

So the next time pay day rolled around,
Big Jim Goff a dollar short was found.
When he asked what for, comes this reply:
"You was docked for the time you spent up in the sky." So...

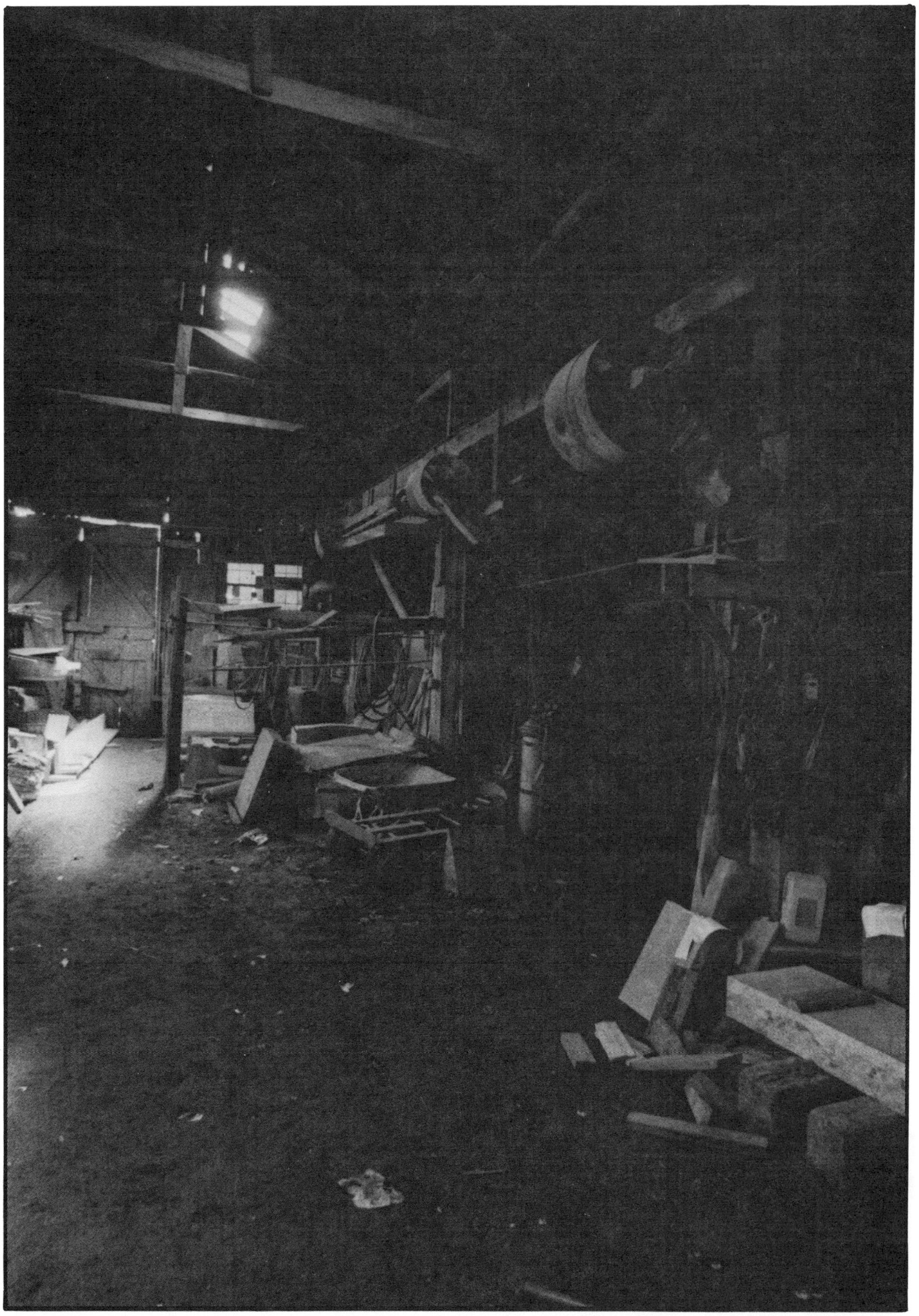

New Dorian Am
(DD A E)
Key of Em

MORNING SONG

Like myself this song needs a couple of cups of coffee to really get perking in the morning.

by Mark Biggs

Harmonic Intro

Ⓐ Slow build to rock rhythm

1.) Sun - rise,   slowly it breaks   Day - break,   softly it peaks
2.) First light,   stir from your sleep   Cock crow,   sit up and speak

Matins,   ring in the day   Greet the new dawn ing,
Morrow,   see with new eyes   Throw off your cov ers,

Ⓑ

good sir awake.   good sir arise.   New day,   don't waste its prom ises.

New age,   wake to your resurrection. New day,

embrace its melody,   Life is for liv ing,   stand up and act.

44

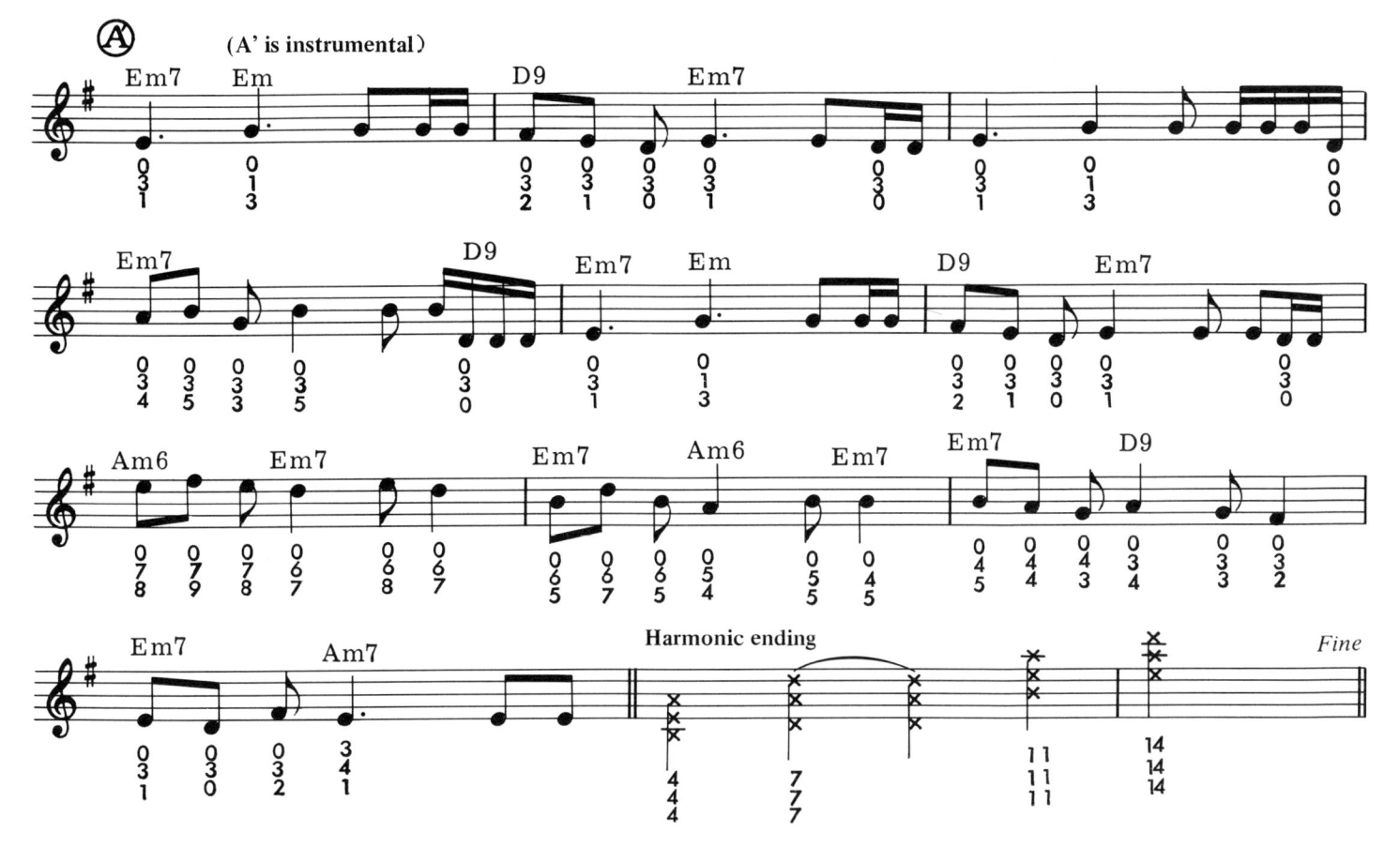

SEQUENCE: INTRO, A, B, A', A, B, A', A into harmonic ending

(Or arrange it as you wish.)

Verses:

3.) Master, there's hay to be mown
    Dear sire, there's sheep to be shorn
    Good Lord, there's fields to be sown
    Leave off your dreaming, good sir good morn.

4.) Husband, your wife begs you please
    Gay sweet, your heart to you prays
    Rascal, get up on your feet
    Stop your pretending, good sir make haste.

5.) Dreamer, your dreams will come true
    Only if you rise to the task.
    Old man, you'll rest soon enough
    Don't lie there sleeping, your moment's not up.

6.) Sunrise, slowly it breaks
    Daybreak, softly it peaks
    Matins, ring in the day
    Greet the new dawning, good sir awake.

Photo by Mark Biggs

SECTION #2

SELECTED SONGS

Most of these songs plus all those from Section #1 are available on a Mel Bay cassette intended to accompany this book.

New Dorian Am
(DD A E)
Key of Em

RAMBLE AWAY

A vagabonding song no doubt played by many a seventeenth century minstrel wandering about the English Midlands. I play it sweet and slow, smoothly rolling like a stroll through those English hills.

Trad. English Folk Song

New Dorian Am
(DD A E)
Key of Em

WHAT DO YOU DO WITH A DRUNKEN SAILOR

Perhaps the best known of the sea chanties. I'm sure that had there been a top 40 pop chart in the 17th century this song would have climbed, or reeled its way to the top.

Trad. English Sea Chantey

Chorus:

Way, hey, and up she rises, (3 times)
Early in the morning.

Verses:

2. Haul him on deck and throw him over, (3 times)
   Early in the morning.
3. Ring him dry until he's sober, etc.
4. Shave his belly with a rusty razor, etc.
5. That's what you do with a drunken sailor, etc.

Mixolydian D
(DD A D)
Key of D

THE LASS OF PATIE'S MILL

A very old Scots tune dating back at least to the early 1700's. It has that old Scottish vim and vigor, so swing to its inner bounce.

Trad. Scottish

Photo by Mark Biggs

POOR WAYFARING STRANGER

Mixolydian D
(DD A D)
Key Em

Trad. American Spiritual

I'm just a poor way-far-ing stranger, A traveling through this world of woe; But there's no sick-ness, sor-row danger, in that bright world to which I'm bound. I'm go-ing there to see my father, I'm go-ing there no more to roam, I'm just a go-ing over Jor-dan, I'm just a go-ing ov-er home.

I know dark clouds will gather 'round me,
I know my way is steep and rough,
But beauteous fields lie just beyond me,
Where souls redeemed their vigil keep.
I'm going there to meet my mother,
She said she'd meet me when I come;
I'm only going over Jordan,
I'm only going over home.

ANDANTE GRAZIOSO

Mixolydian C
(CC G C)

A lovely liquid piece of classical music from the 17th century. It goes along swiftly (andante) in jig time.

Wolfgang Amadeus Mozart

Photo by Mark Biggs

MINUET IN G

Mixolydian D
(DD A D)
Key of G

A classic 17th century dance from one of the baroque masters. Baroque music is exceptionally well suited to the dulcimer because of its frequent use of modes and modal scales. I occasionally like to slip into 4/4 time to give it some swing (this can easily be done by extending the 1st note of the measure by 1 beat.)

J. S. Bach

Photo by Mark Biggs

New Ionian G
(DD G D)
Key of Em

GOD REST YE MERRY GENTLEMEN

This wonderful well known old carol goes well in a straight-forward four time, or jazzed up as you wish. I have given you a couple of bars in six eight time to show you a different sycopation. I personally like to play it nice and gently through a couple of times, then to cut loose and let the <u>merry</u> fly.

Trad. English Carol

MUNGA LATEN

Mixolydian D
(DD A D)

Without a doubt this piece was played on the Swedish humle, that distant ancestor of the mountain dulcimer. It has a distinctly baroque feel to it, and should move smoothly and quickly along its path through the town of Munga.

Trad. Swedish Fiddle Tune

Stately, almost Baroque

THE TOUCHSTONE

Mixolydian D
(DD A D)

This 18th century country dance was named after the alchemist's stone on which he tested the purity of gold. By anybody's calibration it is an 18 karat song at the worst of times. It goes along jauntily, full of sparkle but not too fast.

Trad. English Country Dance

(*) Octave lower pattern substitutes F#m for D at this point.

RAKES OF MALLOW

Mixolydian D
(DD A D)

Mallow was an 18th century seaside resort in Country Cork in the south of Ireland famous or infamous, depending on your point of view, as a place of general merrymaking and spa taking. It goes gaily and unabashed, a little faster than the Touchstone but a perfect companion piece since their melody lines are very similar.

Trad. Irish Country Dance

Bright & Happy

Photo by Max Tyndall

OLD MOLLY HARE

Mixolydian D
(DD A D)

In Scotland this song was known as the Fairy Dance. By the time it had crossed the Atlantic and been processed through Ellis Island its name had been changed to Old Molly Hare. A classic American fiddle tune that's awfully hard to play too fast.

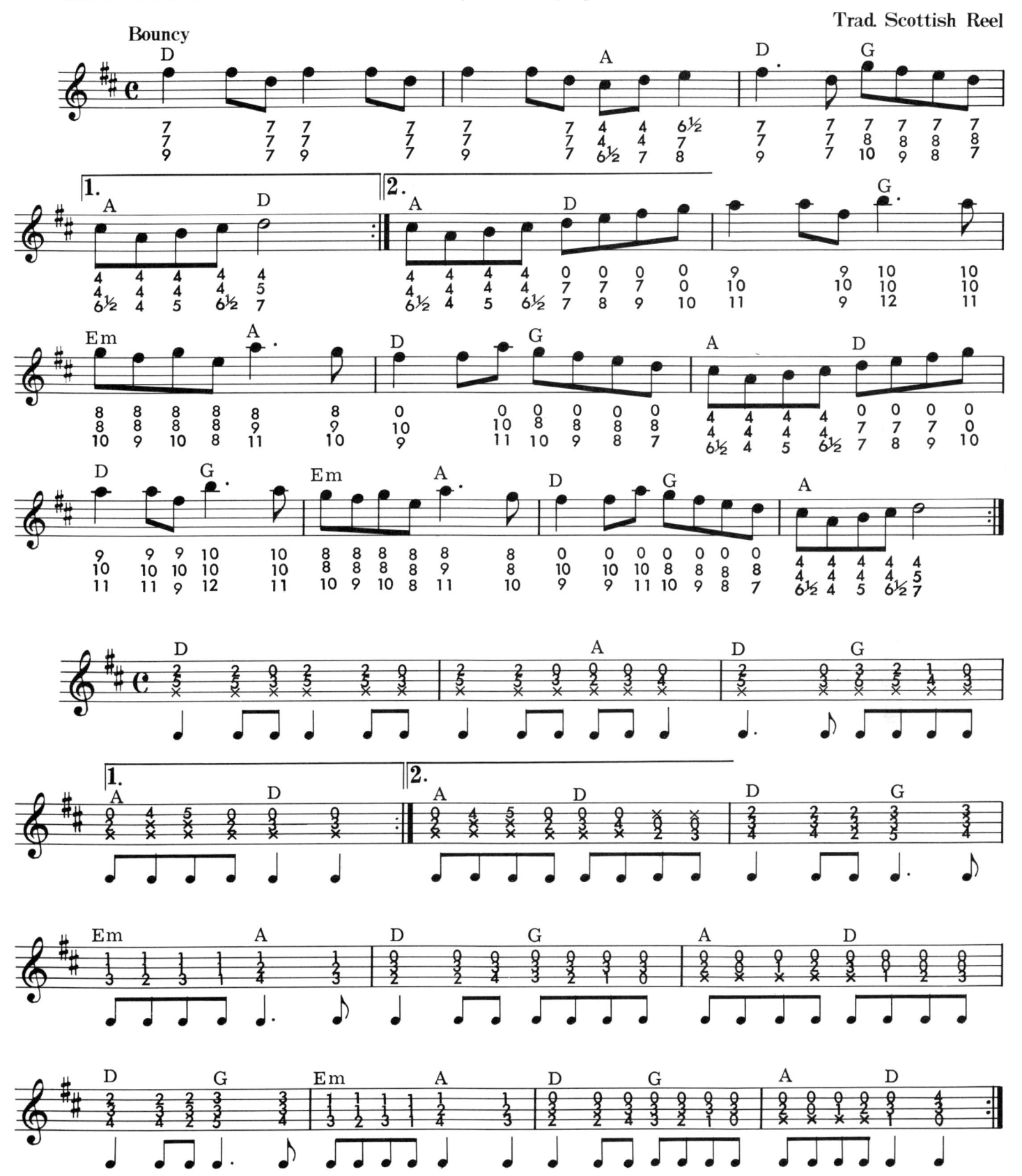

Trad. Scottish Reel

STAR OF COUNTY DOWN

Mixolydian D
(DD A D)
Key of Bm

Also known as "When a Man's in Love" this beautiful air is sometimes played in 3/4 time. I think it's wonderful played fast or slow, as long as the brogue is retained. Accordingly, on the accompanying cassette I play it first in 3/4, then in 4/4.

Trad. Irish Air

SHEEBEG SHEEMORE

Mixolydian D
(DD A D)

According to Robin Williamson this song was originally called "The Bonney Cuckoo", until it became the melody for O'Carolan's (the most famous of the Irish harpers) first song. Sheebeg and Sheemore were two hills occupied by rival fairy factions, though you would never guess this tension within the song. As beautiful a tune as you're likely to find anywhere; it practically plays itself.

Trad. Irish

Photo by Max Tyndall

GOLDEN HAIRED MAID IN THE MORNING

Mixolydian D
(DD A D)
Key Bm

This piece draws its inspiration, its breath from the Rennaissance. It should flow smoothly, with just a hint of melancholy in it.

by Mark Biggs

Photo by Max Tyndall

Photo by J. Edwin Titus

FAREWELL & ADIEU
(YE FINE DULCIMER PLAYERS)

Playing music is as much the fine art of listening as anything else. Listen to yourself when you play as you would listen to someone whose playing you respect or as you would listen to a favorite record: with careful attention and personal involvement. When you make music with friends, which you should do as often as possible, listen closely to the total sound as well as to your particular contribution. The more you learn to hear the better you will be able to play.

Perseverance is also a key. Your playing will improve if you just stick with it. Try to play every day, if only for half an hour; there's nothing so frustrating and ultimately killing as having to relearn the same basics over and over. When your hands learn their lessons your mind will be free to proceed to new endeavors, and your ears will be free to hear what your heart feels. The end aim of practice is to enable you to play as you feel after all. So obviously (though it took me awhile to figure this out), learn songs which move and please you; they are destined to become an intimate part of your life. The dulcimer being very much a rhythm instrument, I highly encourage you to work with simple rhythm instruments such as spoons, bones, maracas, tin pans, or whatever else you can grab when listening to music (though try to keep at least one hand on the steering wheel). And whatever else you may or may not do, share your knowledge with others, for as Robin Williamson of Incredible String Band fame says, "you can't become less by giving away tunes or ideas." Play to the best of your ability at all times and your ability will steadily expand, as will the enjoyment you derive from playing your mountain dulcimer.

Feel free to write to me at: R.R.#3 Box 367B/ Galena, Mo. 65656 (be sure to enclose a stamped self-addressed envelope). I'll answer all letters just as soon as I can. Meanwhile, keep playing.

GLOSSARY OF SOME IMPORTANT TERMS AND SYMBOLS

Harmonics: clear bell-like tones produced when you lightly touch (just barely rest your finger on) the string at one of the dulcimer's nodes (3rd, 4th, 7th, 11th, 14th frets) and strike the string. This will take some practice, and you may find that in time louder harmonics can be produced by striking the string and pulling your finger off a fraction of a second later. In this book, harmonics are indicated by x's appearing on the bar staff. (See intro to Morning Song, p.44)

Hammer-on: this occurs when you strike a note and then bring down your finger on a note above the original. For instance, pluck the melody string while fretting it at the third fret with your second finger and immediately 'hammer' your index finger down on the fourth fret.

Pull-Off: occurs when you strike a note and pull off your noting finger (plucking the string as much as possible) so that a note fretted below the original note may subsequently ring out. *Note: a very nice effect is created by a series of hammer-ons and pull-offs, such as can be heard in Tomorrow Today.

Slide: occurs when you strike a note and move to a higher or lower note without removing the fretted finger from the fretboard, thus sliding your finger to the next note.

Tie: ⌒ or ⌣ means that you hold two notes joined by this symbol for the combined time indicated; i.e. the two become one note.

‖: :‖ when you see this configuration enclosing a passage it means you are to repeat that passage before proceeding on.

Fine: (pronounced 'feen') means 'the end'.

Ritard: slow down, fade out.

READING TIME VALUES

Time Signatures occur directly after the treble clef (𝄞) symbol and tell you how to count the song; i.e. how many beats each measure will receive. Here are some common signatures:

C or 4/4 = four beats per measure (Typical reel) Count: 1,2,3,4

3/4 = three beats (Standard waltz or minuet time.) Count: 1,2,3/1,2,3.

2/4 = two beats (Standard polka.) Count: 1,2/1,2.

6/4 = six beats, counted: 1,2,3,4,5,6/1,2,3,4,5,6.

6/8 = six beats, usually grouped in two sets of three, counted:
1,2,3; 1,2,3/1,2,3; 1,2,3. (Typical jig.)

12/8 = twelve beats, usually grouped as four sets of three, counted:
1,2,3; 1,2,3; 1,2,3; 1,2,3/1,2,3; 1,2,3; 1,2,3; 1,2,3.
(Typical slide.)

Note values, the time alloted to a single note, are as follows:

𝅝 = whole note; receives 4 beats.

𝅗𝅥 = half note; receives 2 beats.

𝅘𝅥 = quarter note; receives 1 beat

𝅘𝅥𝅮 = eighth note; receives ½ beat, or half the time of a quarter note.

𝅘𝅥𝅯 = sixtenth note; ½ of an eighth note (𝅘𝅥𝅮), or ¼ of a quarter note.

A dotted note receives half again as long a count as its note value.

Rests receive the following counts:

▬ = whole note rest;   ▬ = half note rest;   𝄽 = quarter note rest;

𝄾 = eighth note rest

Triplets: a group of three notes played in the equivalent time of two notes of the same kind.

Counting the rhythm of a measure: Part of the secret to playing a dulcimer, or any instrument, is to get your foot tapping out a steady rhythm in the correct time signature. Here are a few measures portrayed using a verbal count to help you join note value with the basic time.

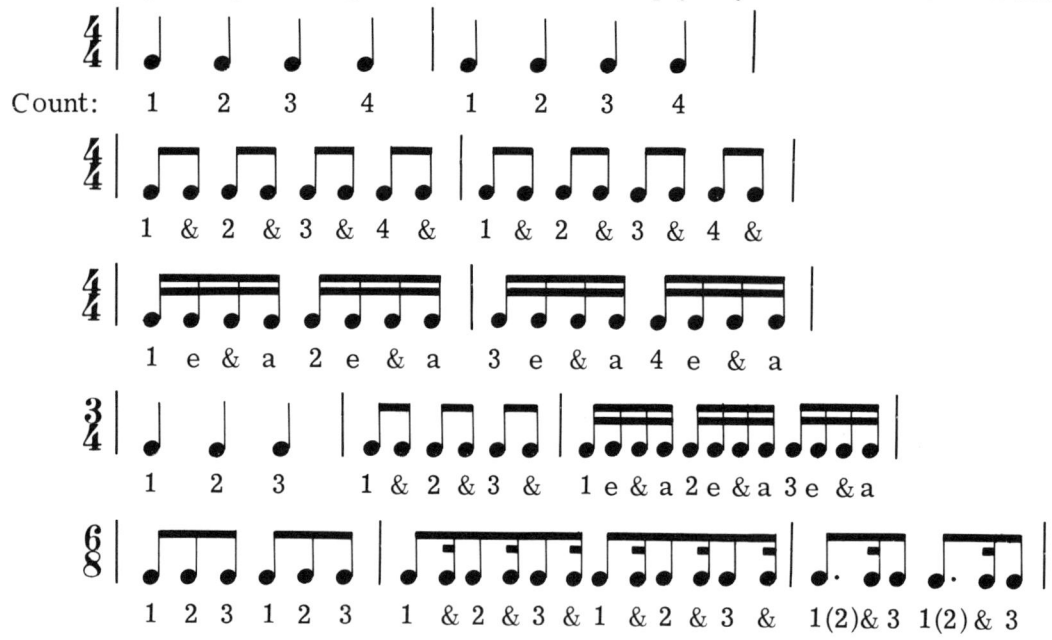

Count: 1 2 3 4 1 2 3 4

1 & 2 & 3 & 4 & 1 & 2 & 3 & 4 &

1 e & a 2 e & a 3 e & a 4 e & a

1 2 3 1 & 2 & 3 & 1 e & a 2 e & a 3 e & a

1 2 3 1 2 3 1 & 2 & 3 & 1 & 2 & 3 & 1(2)& 3 1(2)& 3

Let's mix it up a little by looking at a few less regular examples: From the first three measures of The Lass Of Patie's Mill:

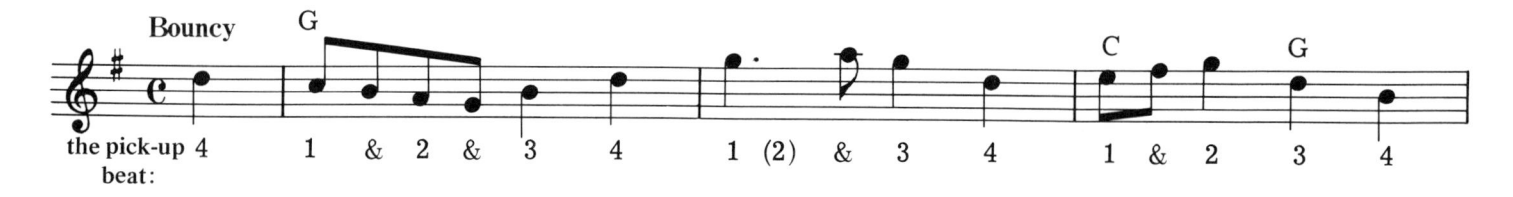

the pick-up 4   1 & 2 & 3 4   1 (2) & 3   4   1 & 2   3   4
beat:

And from the first three bars of Sheebeg Sheemore:

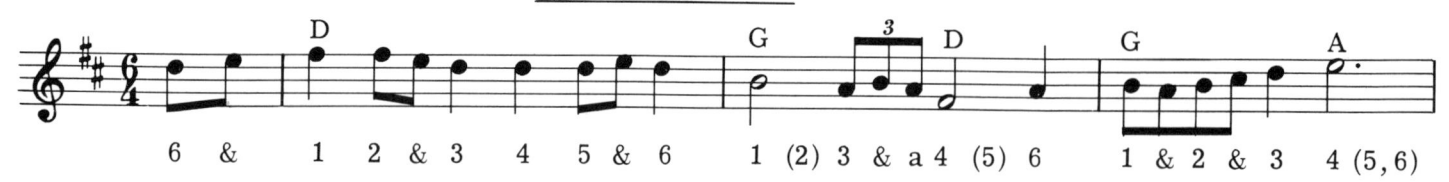

6 &   1 2 & 3 4 5 & 6   1 (2) 3 & a 4 (5) 6   1 & 2 & 3   4 (5,6)

And finally from the first three bars of Peppermint Stick Rag:

1 (&) a 2 & (3) & 4   1 (&) a 2 & (3) & 4   1 (&) a 2 & (3) & 4

70

Sharps and Flats in the Keys of:

C= no sharps or flats

G= F♯   F= B♭

D= F♯, C♯   B♭ = B♭, E♭

A= F♯, C♯, G♯   E♭ = B♭, E♭, A♭

E= F♯, C♯, G♯, D♯   A♭ = B♭, E♭, A♭, D♭

B= F♯, C♯, G♯, D♯, A♯   D♭ = B♭, E♭, A♭, D♭, G♭

F♯= F♯, C♯, G♯, D♯, A♯, E♯

You may find it handy to know what notes make up which chords
When you wish to figure out fingering patterns and chords not
given in the following charts.

```
C= C, E, G                F= F, A, C              B= B, D♯, F♯
C7= C, E, G, B♭           F7= F, A, C, D♯         B7= B, D♯, F♯, A
Cm= C, D♯, G              Fm= F, G♯, C            Bm= B, D, F♯
Cm7= C, D♯, G, B          Fm7= F, G♯, C, D♯       Bm7= B, D, F♯, A
Cm6= C, D♯, G, A

C♯ = C♯, G♯, F            F♯= F♯, A♯, C♯
C♯7 = C♯, G♯, F, B        F♯7= F♯, A♯, C♯, E
C♯m = C♯, G♯, E           F♯m= F♯, A, C♯
C♯m7= C♯, G♯, E, B        F♯m7= F♯, A, C♯, E
C♯m6= C♯, G♯, E, A♯

D= D, F♯, A               G= G, B, D
D7= D, F♯, A, C           G7= G, B, D, F
Dm= D, F, A               Gm= G, B♭, D
Dm7= D, F, A, C           Gm7= G, B♭, D, F
Dm6= D, F, A, B

E= E, G♯, B               A= A, C♯, E
E7= E, G♯, B, D           A7= A, C♯, E, G
Em= E, G, B               Am= A, C, E
Em7= E, G, B, D           Am7= A, C, E, G
```

Here are a couple of common chord patterns:

```
I    IV   V    VIm           I    VIm    IIm7    V7
C,   F,   G,   Am            C,   Am,    Dm7,    G7
G,   C,   D,   Em            G,   Em,    Am7,    D7
D,   G,   A,   Bm            D,   Bm,    Em7,    A7
A,   D,   E,   Fm            A,   F♯m,   Bm7,    E7
E,   A,   B,   Cm            E,   C♯m,   F♯m7,   B7
```

MIXOLYDIAN MODE: CHORDS FOR KEY OF D ∗ (C & E)

(Key D/ Key C/ Key E)
(DD A D: CC G C: EE B E)

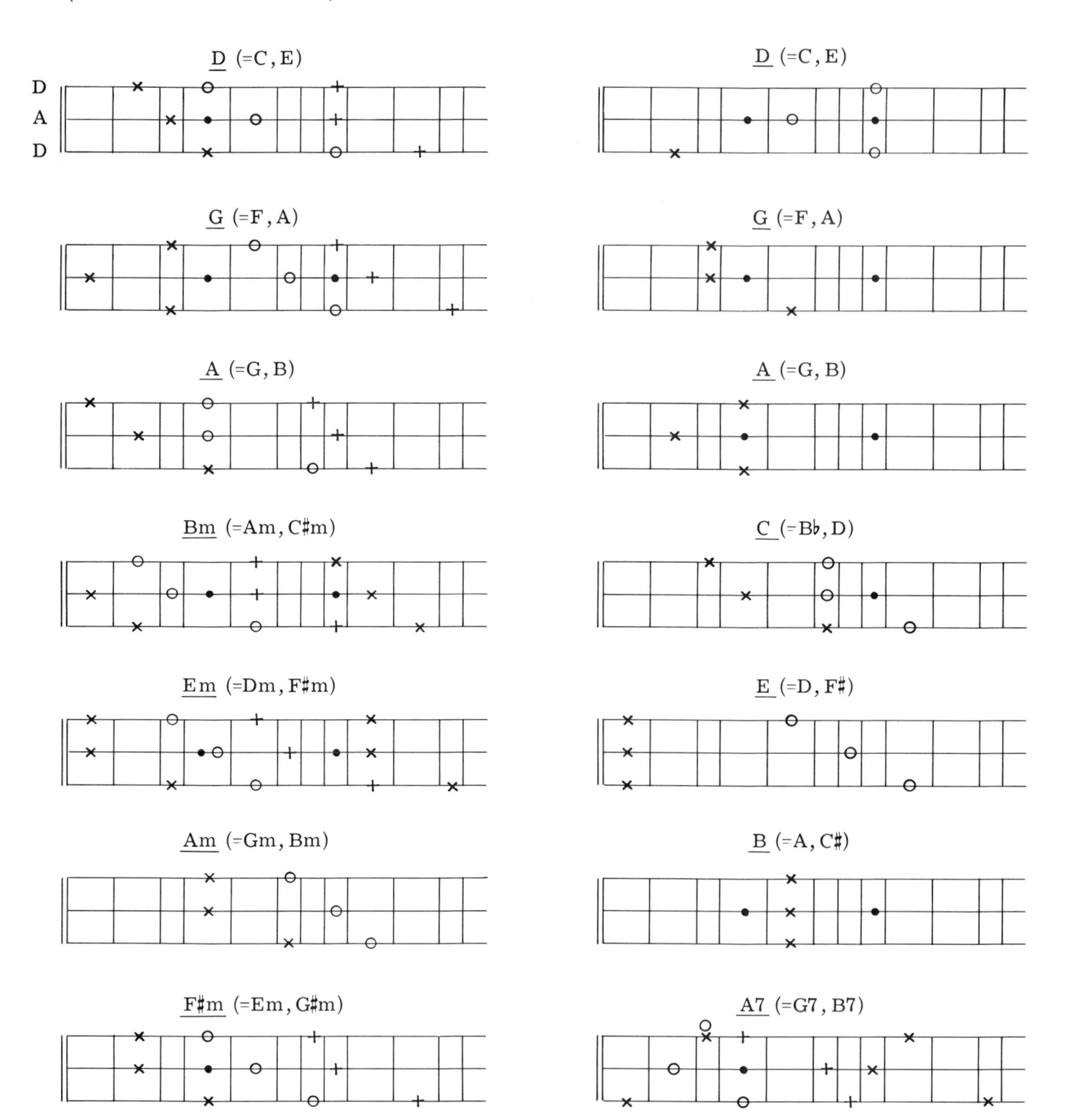

D
A
D

D (=C, E)   D (=C, E)

G (=F, A)   G (=F, A)

A (=G, B)   A (=G, B)

Bm (=Am, C♯m)   C (=B♭, D)

Em (=Dm, F♯m)   E (=D, F♯)

Am (=Gm, Bm)   B (=A, C♯)

F♯m (=Em, G♯m)   A7 (=G7, B7)

∗Read symbols (+, ○, ×) as a group from right to left to make a chord. Each group makes up one possible fingering pattern equivalent to the full chord indicated. No partial chords are included here.

∗∗Two important ideas must be understood here. One, with all chords in the Mixolydian mode the bass note and the melody note may be inverted (i.e., positions exchanged) and the chord remains the same. Two, fingerings

MIXOLYDIAN MODE: CHORDS FOR KEY OF D ∗ (C & E)

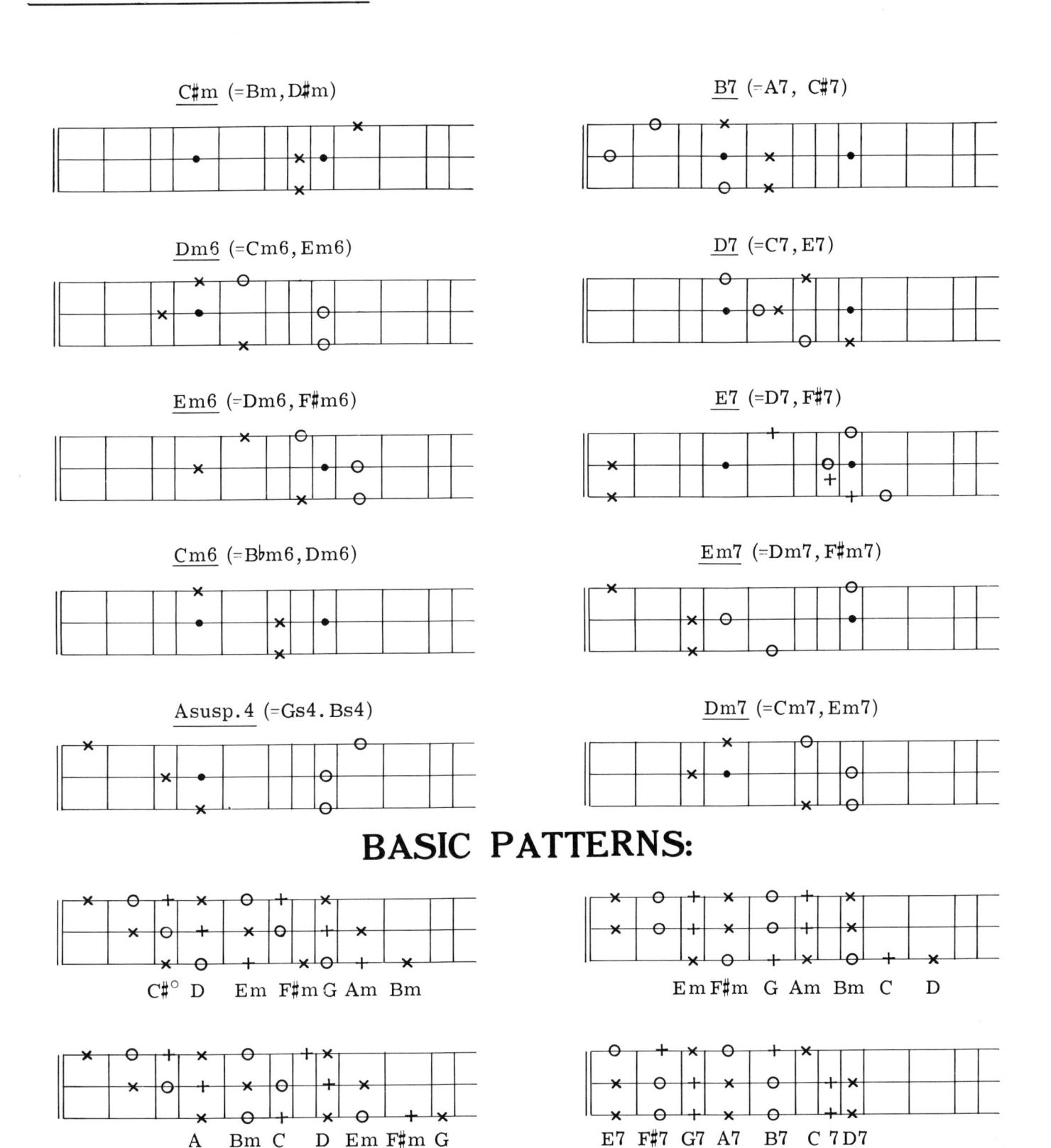

C♯m (=Bm, D♯m)

B7 (=A7, C♯7)

Dm6 (=Cm6, Em6)

D7 (=C7, E7)

Em6 (=Dm6, F♯m6)

E7 (=D7, F♯7)

Cm6 (=B♭m6, Dm6)

Em7 (=Dm7, F♯m7)

Asusp.4 (=Gs4, Bs4)

Dm7 (=Cm7, Em7)

BASIC PATTERNS:

C♯° D Em F♯m G Am Bm

Em F♯m G Am Bm C D

A Bm C D Em F♯m G

E7 F♯7 G7 A7 B7 C7 D7

remain the same when you are tuned in different keys; only the name of the chord changes relative to the key you're in. I have indicated in parenthesis the new chord names for the same fingerings when you change from the key of D to the keys of C and E.

73

NEW IONIAN MODE-KEY OF G (F & A)

(Key G/ Key F/ Key A)
(DD G D: CC F C: EE A E)

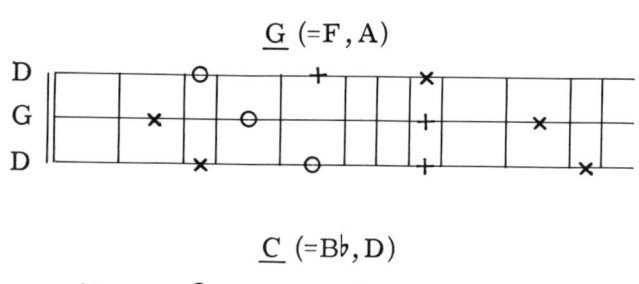

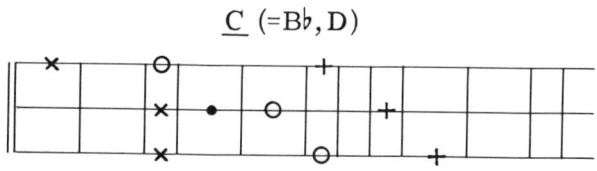

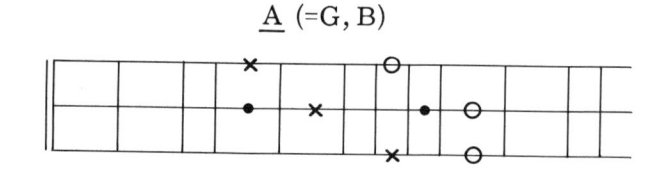

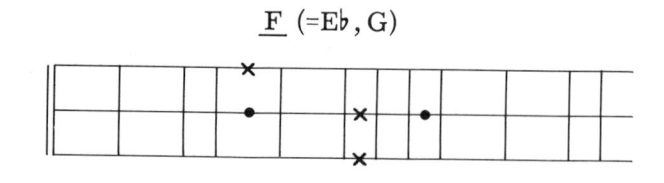

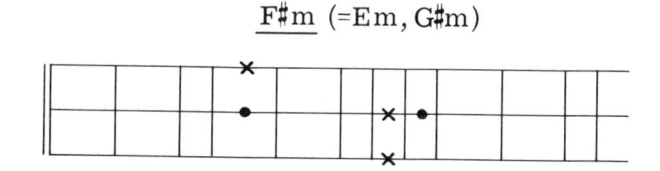

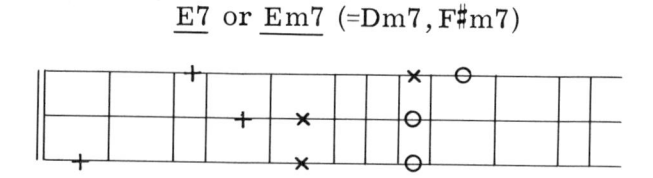

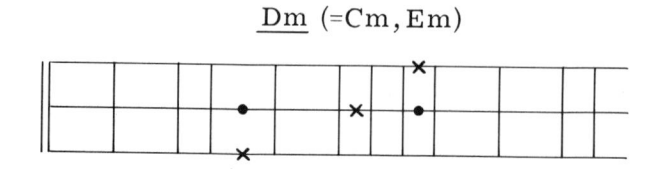

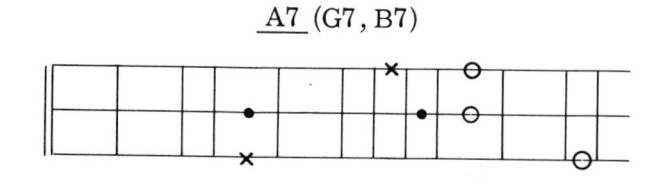

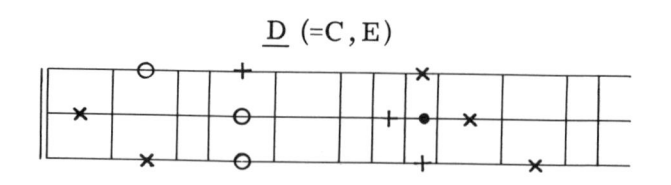

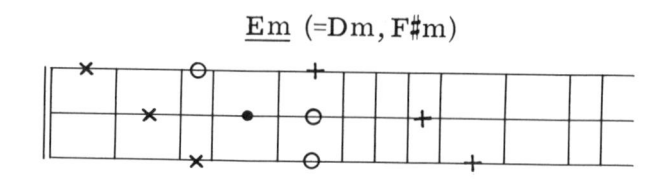

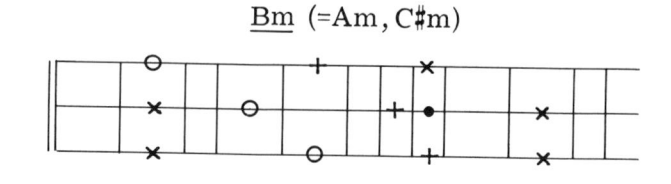

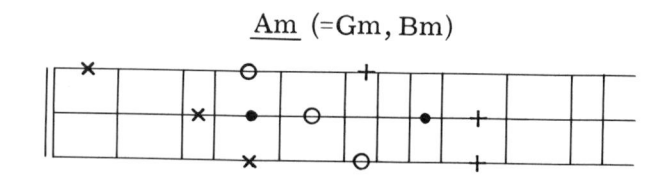

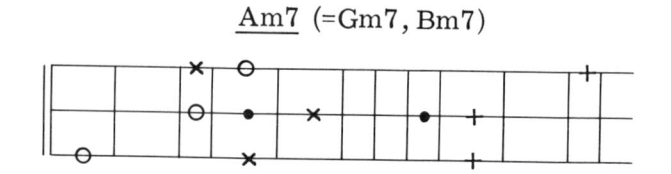

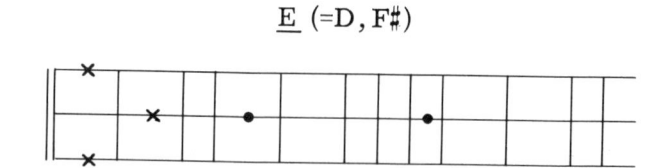

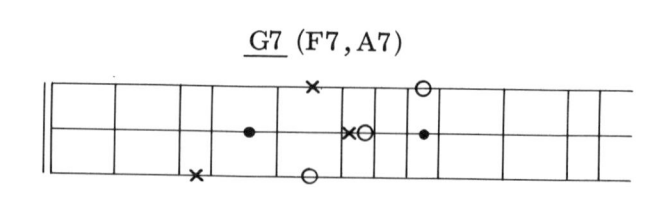

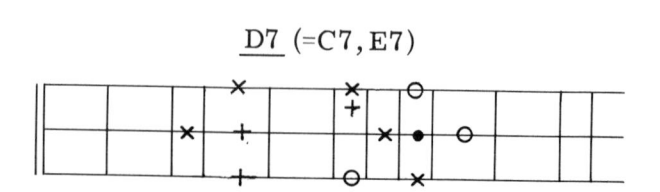

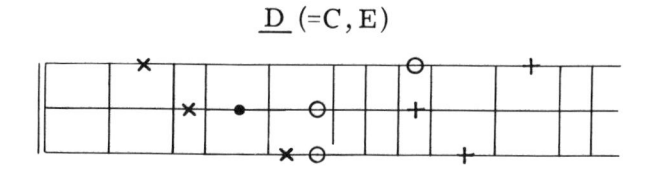

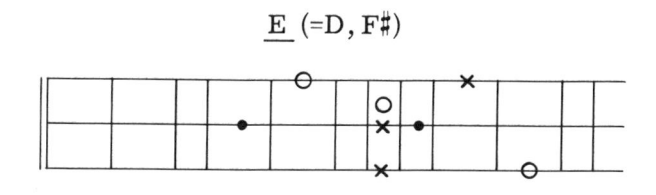

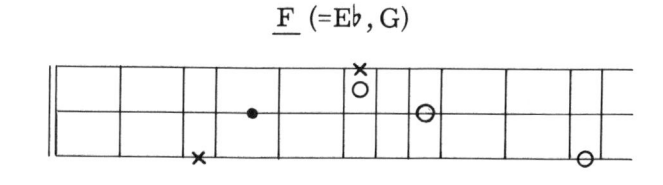

AEOLIAN MODE: CHORDS FOR KEY OF DM (CM, EM)
(Key Dm/ Cm/ Em)
(CC A D: B♭ B♭ G C: DD B E)

Dm (=Cm, Em)

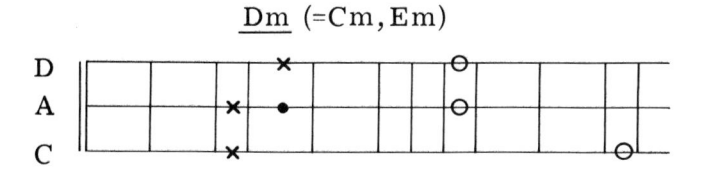

D (=C, E)

Em (=Dm, F♯m)

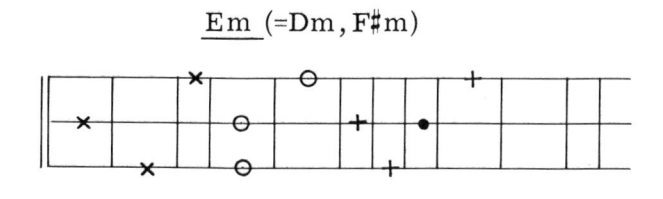

E (=D, F♯)

F♯m (=Em, G♯m)

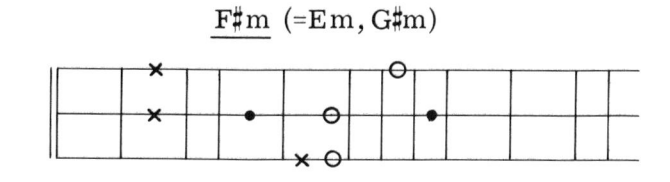

F (=E♭, G)

Gm (=Fm, Am)

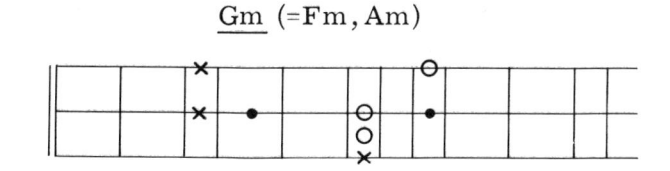

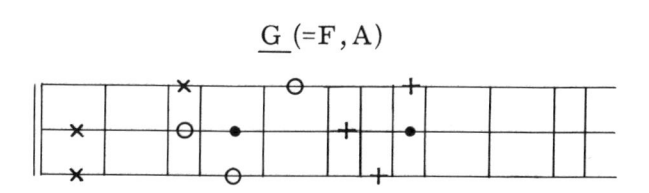

G (=F, A)

Am (=Gm, Bm)

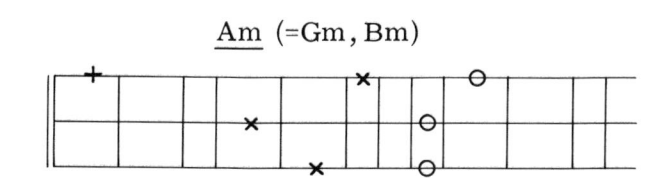

A (=G, B)

Bm (=Am, C♯m)

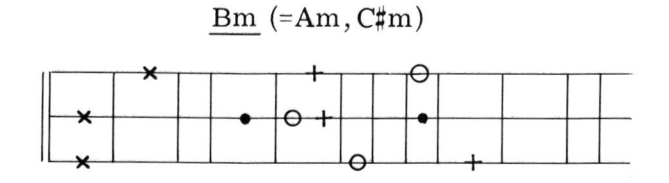

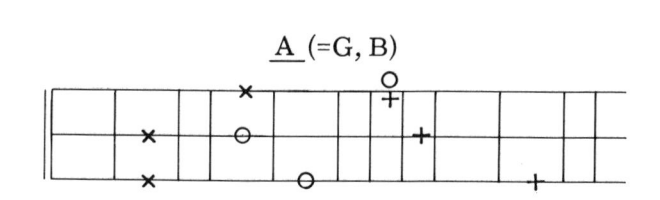

B (=A, C♯) (partial)

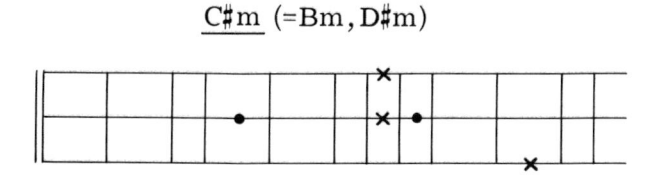

C♯m (=Bm, D♯m)

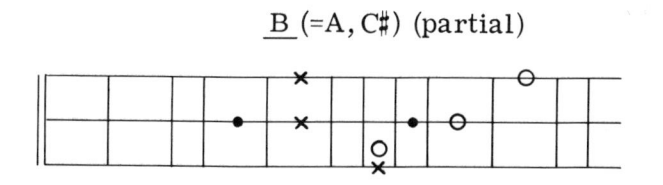

C (=B♭, D)

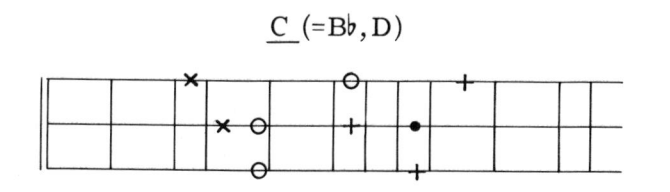

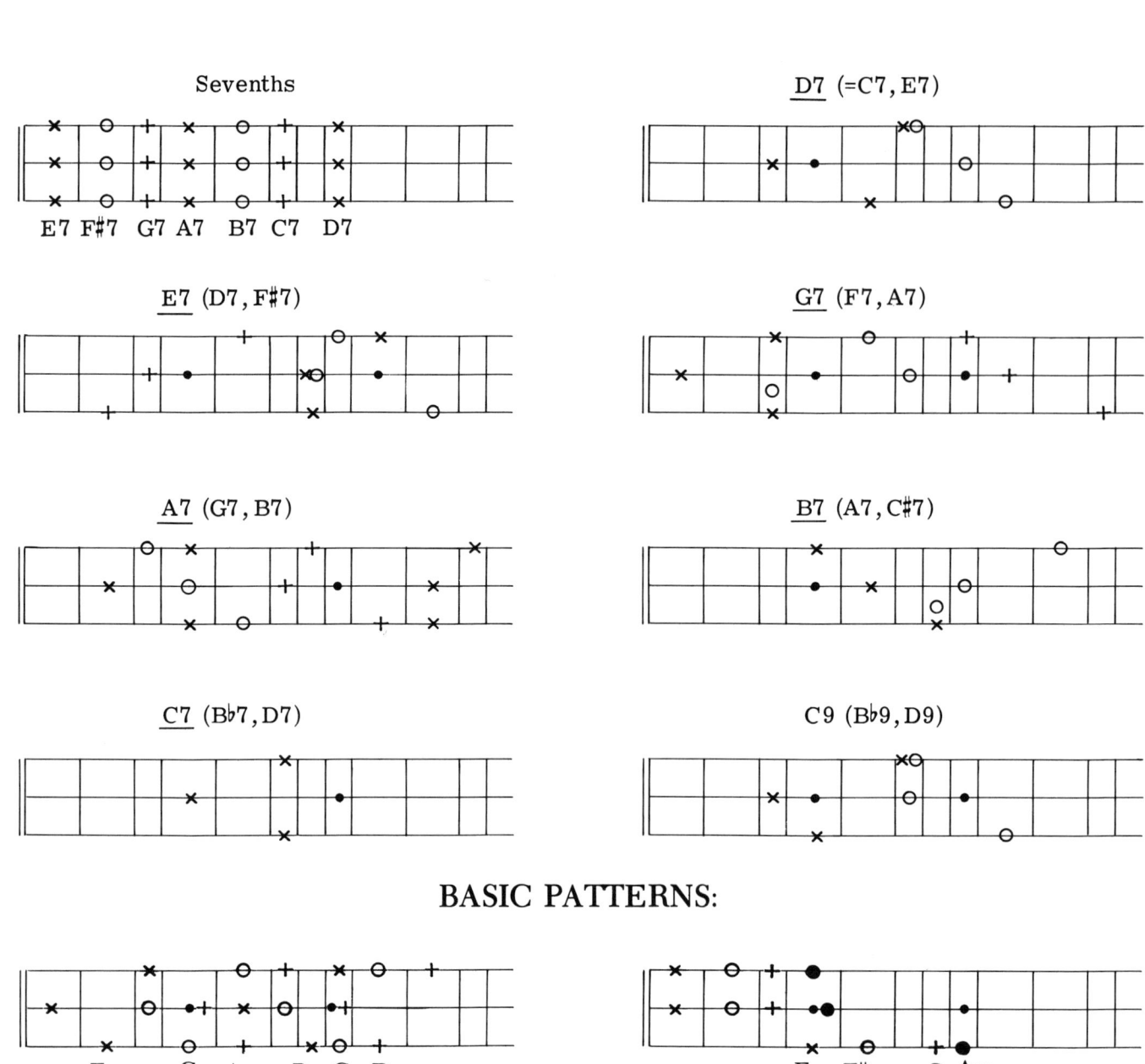

AEOLIAN MODE: CHORDS FOR KEY OF DM (CM, EM)

Sevenths

E7 F#7 G7 A7 B7 C7 D7

D7 (=C7, E7)

E7 (D7, F#7)

G7 (F7, A7)

A7 (G7, B7)

B7 (A7, C#7)

C7 (B♭7, D7)

C9 (B♭9, D9)

BASIC PATTERNS:

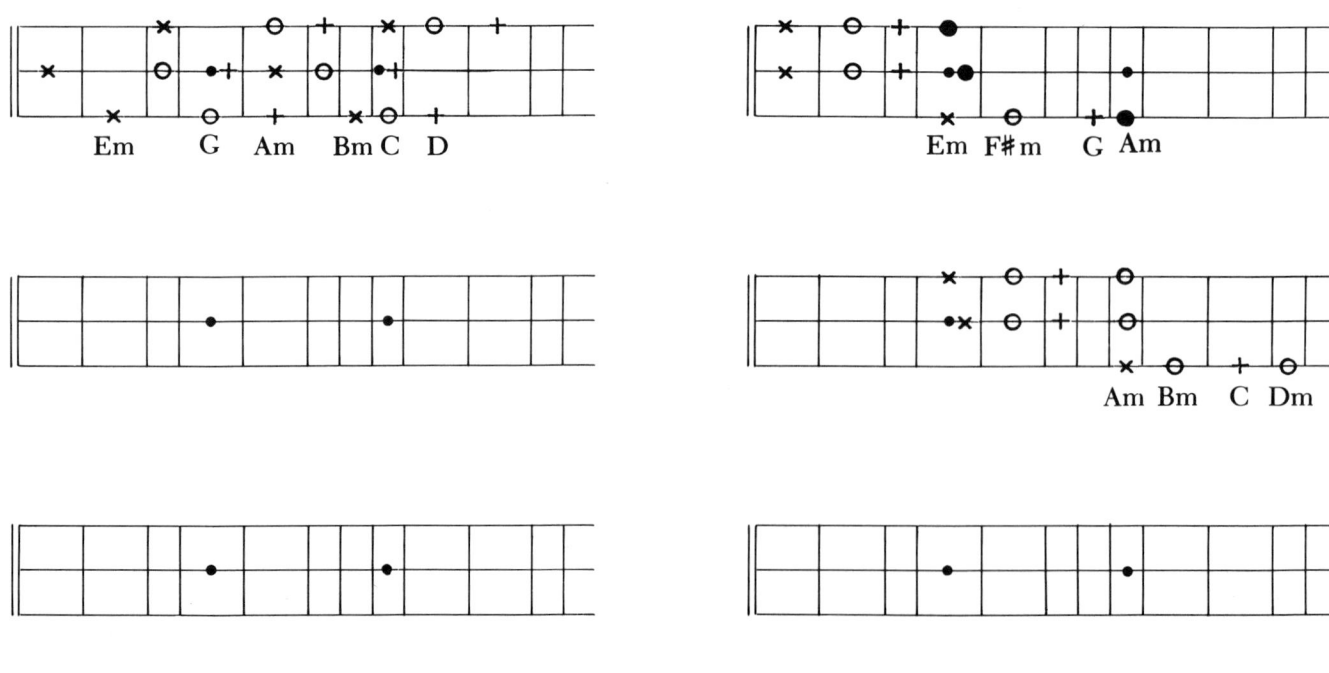

Em G Am Bm C D

Em F#m G Am

Am Bm C Dm

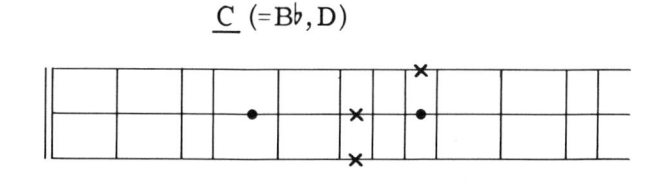

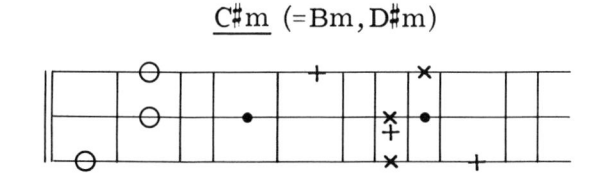

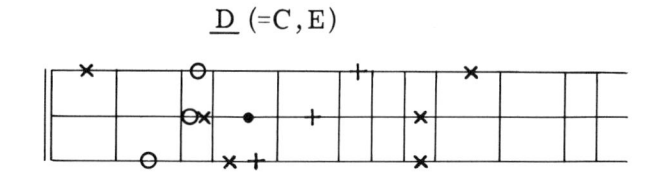

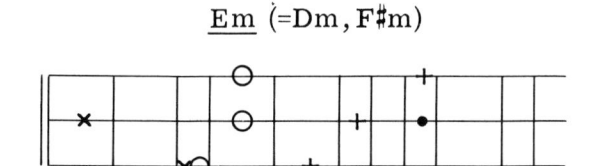

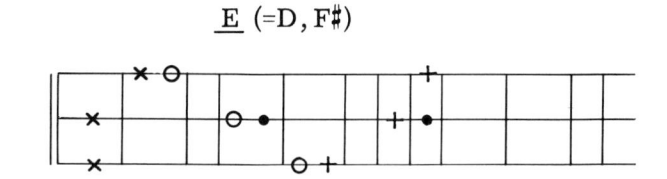

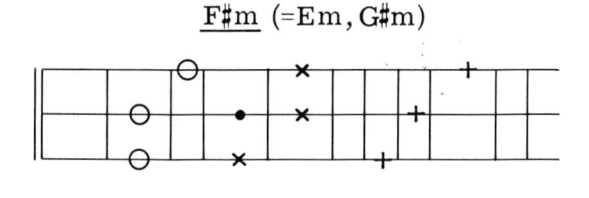

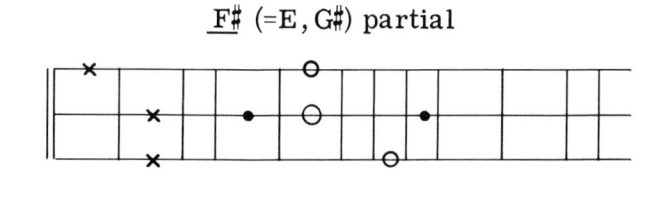

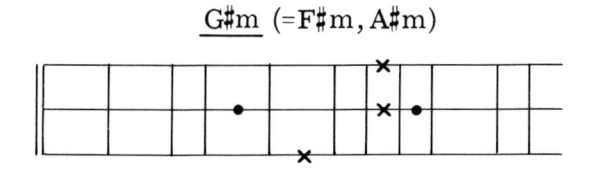

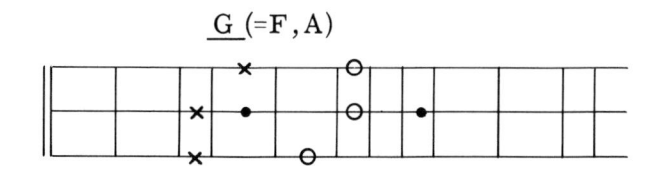

NEW DORIAN MODE: CHORDS FOR THE KEY OF AM (GM, BM)

(Key Am/ Gm/ Bm)
(DD A E: CC G D: EE B F#)

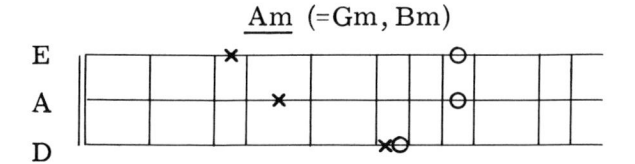

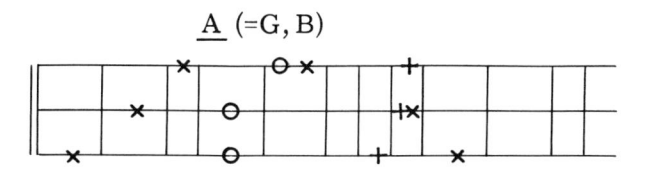

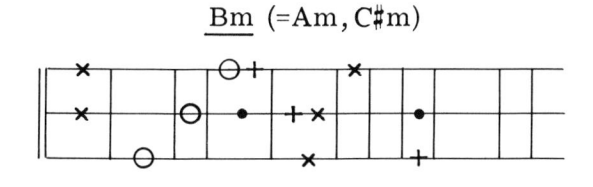

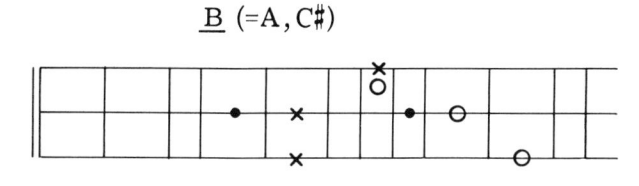

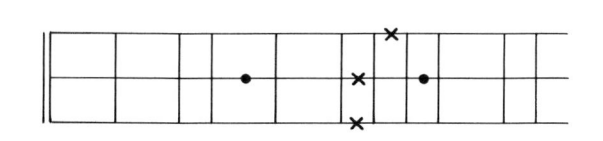

NEW DORIAN MODE: CHORDS FOR KEY OF AM (GM, BM)

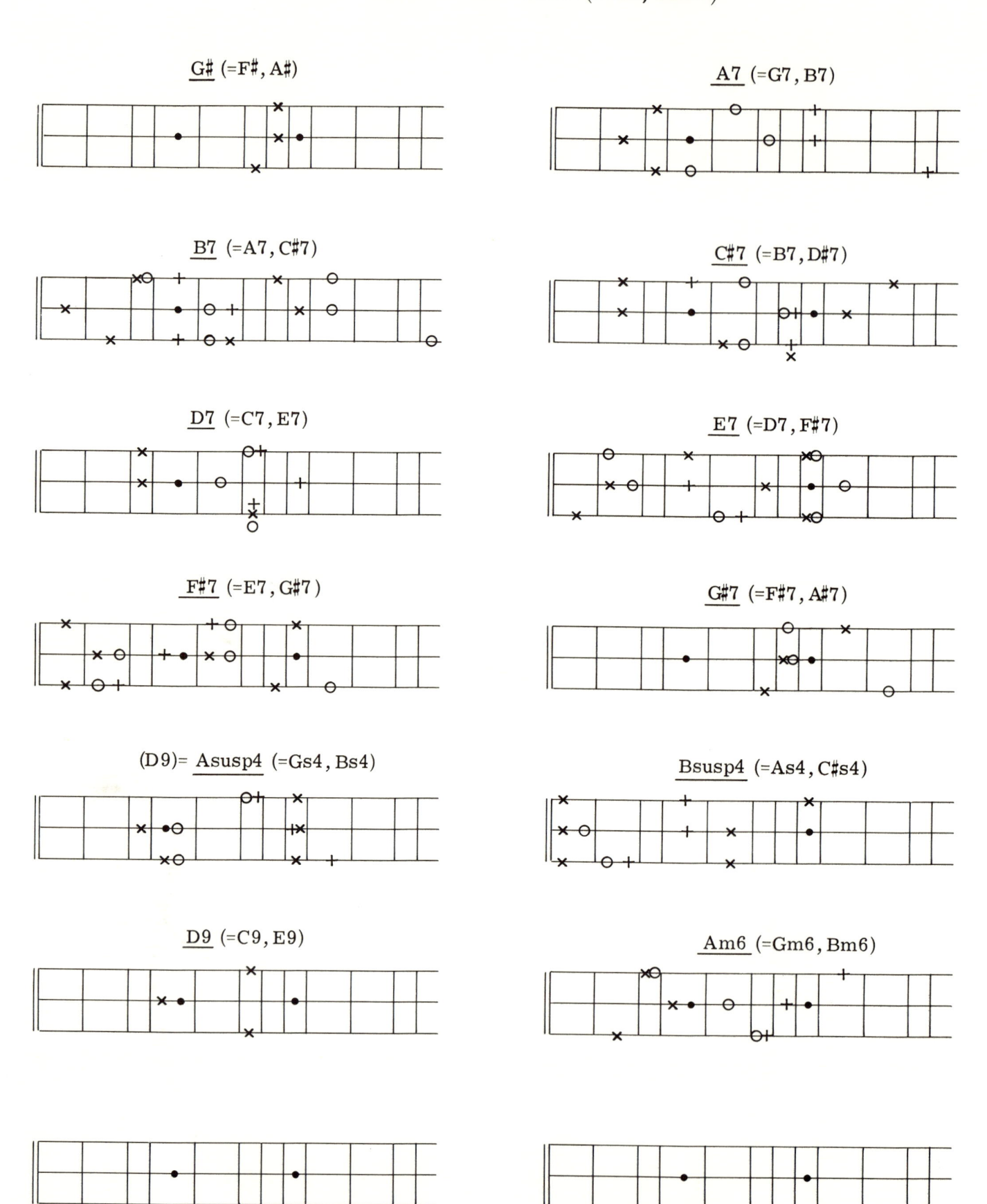

G# (=F#, A#)

A7 (=G7, B7)

B7 (=A7, C#7)

C#7 (=B7, D#7)

D7 (=C7, E7)

E7 (=D7, F#7)

F#7 (=E7, G#7)

G#7 (=F#7, A#7)

(D9)= Asusp4 (=Gs4, Bs4)

Bsusp4 (=As4, C#s4)

D9 (=C9, E9)

Am6 (=Gm6, Bm6)

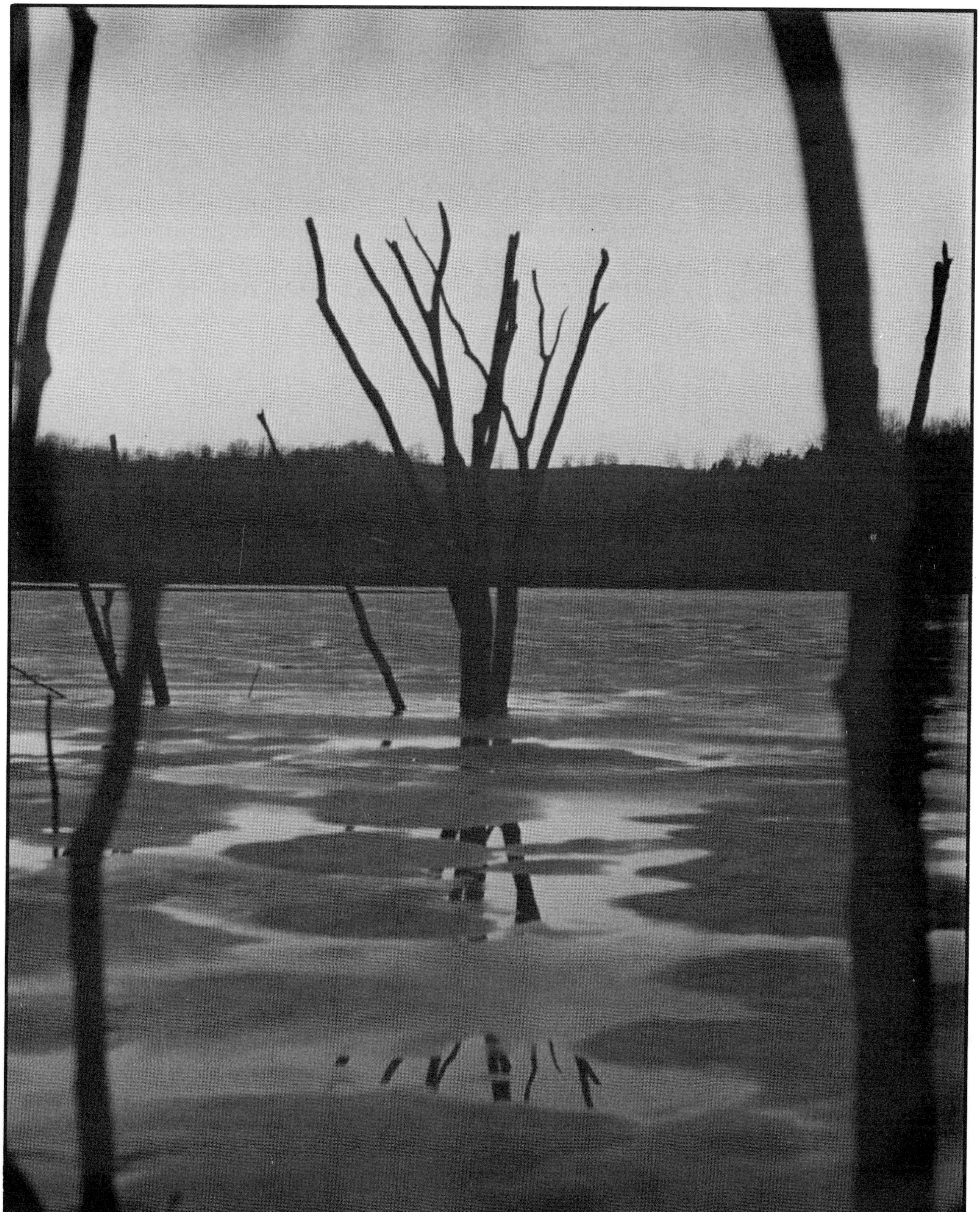

MEL BAY

Everybody's Music Teacher